The Deep End

ISBN 9781788125642

Cover image © Shutterstock
Typeset in Garamond Premier Pro
Printed by Hussar Books

Messenger Publications,
37 Leeson Place, Dublin D02 E5V0
www.messenger.ie

The Deep End

A Journey with the Sunday Gospels in the Year of Matthew

Tríona Doherty & Jane Mellett

Foreword by Jessie Rogers

About the Authors

Tríona Doherty and Jane Mellett got to know each other when they both took an undergraduate degree in Theology in St Patrick's College, Maynooth (1998–2001). They both also completed their Masters in Theology (with a specialisation in Scripture) in 2003. From 2011 to 2021, they together composed 'The Deep End' reflections for *Intercom*. In 2021 they published their first book together, *The Deep End: A Journey with the Sunday Gospels in the Year of Luke*.

Tríona Doherty is editor of *Reality* magazine. As a writer and editor, she has contributed to Redemptorist Communications, CatholicIreland.net, Messenger Publications and the Carmelite Institute of Britain and Ireland. She has also worked on various projects with Good Shepherd Ireland and Laudato Si' Movement. Tríona worked in regional journalism for more than ten years, most recently with the *Westmeath Independent*. Originally from Kells, Co. Meath, she lives in Athlone with her husband and seven-year-old son.

Jane Mellett is the Laudato Si' Officer for Trócaire and also works with the Laudato Si' Movement. Her role in both organisations involves exploring how faith communities can respond to the environmental crises. Prior to this she was a parish pastoral worker in the Archdiocese of Dublin and has worked in the area of pastoral ministry for over ten years. A native of Carlow, Jane is a qualified spiritual director, yoga teacher and retreat facilitator. She writes for a number of publications including the *Laudato Si'* column in *The Irish Catholic* and has contributed to *Reality* and *Messenger* magazines.

Acknowledgements

This series of books began its life several years ago when we both attended a conference in St Patrick's College Maynooth. There we met then editor of *Intercom*, Francis Cousins, who asked us to take on the writing of a series of reflections on the Sunday Gospel readings, entitled 'The Deep End'. This series of books would not have come into being without this initial invitation. We would like to thank Francis and the subsequent editors of *Intercom*.

We would also like to thank all those who supported *A Journey with the Sunday Gospels in the Year of Luke*.

It has been a pleasure to once again work with Fr Donal Neary SJ and the team at Messenger Publications, in particular Carolanne Henry, Kate Kiernan, Paula Nolan and Cecilia West.

We would like to sincerely thank Dr Jessie Rogers, Dean of the Faculty of Theology and Lecturer in Sacred Scripture, St Patrick's Pontifical University, Maynooth, for her uplifting words in the foreword.

A heartfelt thank you to our friends Angela Hanley, Nóirin Lynch, Olivia Maher and Sylvia Thompson, who read early drafts and offered insightful and constructive feedback.

A special debt of gratitude goes to Rev. Dr Brendan McConvery CSsR, retired Lecturer in Sacred Scripture, St Patrick's College Maynooth, and Fr Séamus O'Connell, Professor of Sacred Scripture, St Patrick's College Maynooth. Ever since our first year studying theology in St Patrick's College Maynooth and through our postgraduate studies, they have inspired our love of Scripture and continue to break open the Word for many people across this island.

Finally, thank you to our families, in particular Mary and Cahir Doherty, Pat and Samuel Doyle, and Margaret and Gerry Mellett, for their constant support.

❧ CONTENTS ❧

Foreword .... ❧   8

1: Welcome .... ❧   12

2: Advent .... ❧   22

3: Christmas .... ❧   34

4: Ordinary Time (1) .... ❧   48

5: Lent .... ❧   62

6: Easter .... ❧   76

7: Ordinary Time (2) .... ❧   100

7.1: Season of Creation .... ❧   132

Index of Scripture References .... ❧   164

Foreword

In the apostolic letter instituting the Sunday of the Word of God, Pope Francis wrote:

> The relationship between the Risen Lord, the community of believers and sacred Scripture is essential to our identity as Christians. Without the Lord who opens our minds to them, it is impossible to understand the Scriptures in depth. Yet the contrary is equally true: without the Scriptures, the events of the mission of Jesus and of his Church in this world would remain incomprehensible.

Reading Scripture, encountering Jesus and growing as missionary disciples are intricately related. What is needed are ways to make the Gospel come alive for people in a way that speaks into the ordinariness and wonder of their lives. I am reminded of the story in Acts where the Holy Spirit orchestrates a meeting between Philip and an Ethiopian official on the desert road to Gaza. Philip asks, 'Do you understand what you are reading?' The reply is poignant: 'How can I, unless someone guides me?' (Acts 8:30–31).

This is where *The Deep End* comes in. It is a gentle yet sure-footed guide to a life-giving encounter with the Sunday gospel readings for the year in which Matthew is proclaimed. If you are wondering whether there is room in the market for another resource aimed at unpacking the Sunday gospels, my answer is that there is definitely room for *this* one. The authors' perspectives are fresh, kind but challenging, and they open the Scriptures in a way that beckons toward growth by attraction, not by preaching or laying guilt trips on anyone. Jane and Tríona understand that genuine transformation is invitational. It takes the path, not of 'shoulds' and 'oughts', but of free response to God and others and the opening of ourselves to love.

Sitting with their reflections, I found myself longing to be the kind of disciple that Matthew's Jesus invites us to be. And it was a desire that felt like the beginning of a joyful adventure. That, to my mind, is what St Ignatius of Loyola meant by the work of the good spirit. The 'Going Deeper' section at the end of each reflection provides stepping stones for the journey. It offers questions and prompts that are simultaneously open-ended and incisive. No vague platitudes here! They are genuine invitations to consider how some of what happens in the story also happens in our lives.

Jane and Tríona work from an interconnected vision of the world in which inner and outer, physical and psychological, sacred and mundane, individual and communal are woven into a holistic vision of life. Their concern for climate and social justice – faithful response to the cry of the earth and the cry of those made poor – resonated particularly strongly with me, as did their perceptive highlighting of the 'third way' that is integral to Jesus' ethics in Matthew's Gospel and so essential for our warring, polarised world to rediscover. Sometimes bible reading and reflection can become quite individual and 'spiritualised'. Tríona and Jane are not going to allow us to fall into that trap. They help us see the connections between faith and life, both the big questions and the nitty gritty of the everyday.

I love the way that the book intentionally follows the circle of the Church year. There are short introductions to Advent, Christmas, Ordinary Time, Lent and Easter. The design of the book harnesses the wisdom of the Church as reflected in both the liturgical calendar and the lectionary to support the reader on his or her faith pilgrimage. It is an ideal support to those of us who long, week by week, to meet Christ in the Liturgy of the Word.

I hope that *The Deep End*'s readers include those who prepare reflections and homilies. It is just the kind of book to anchor a faith-sharing group or to be used by friends or couples who want to grow in their discipleship. It is a great resource for parishes who want to support faith development that is rooted in Scripture. And of course, it is ideal for the individual who wants to journey more intentionally with Jesus. *The Deep End: A Journey with the Sunday Gospels in the Year of Matthew* is not a book to read cover-to-cover in a couple of sittings. It will become a trusted friend, probably alongside a journal, on a year-long pilgrimage with Matthew's Jesus.

Jessie Rogers, Dean of the Faculty of Theology,
St Patrick's Pontifical University, Maynooth

June 2022

❧ 1 ❧

Welcome

'Blessed are the merciful' (Mt 5:7)

Welcome to the second book in *The Deep End* series! It gives us great pleasure to be able to write that sentence: just two years ago, as we started work on our first book, *A Journey with the Sunday Gospels in the Year of Luke*, we were new to the publishing process and unsure as to how it would all come together. But come together it did, thanks to the terrific team at Messenger Publications, and we are delighted with the positive response it's received over the past year. That first book was very much a 'lockdown project', compiled at the height of the Covid-19 pandemic. The writing of this book, however, had to compete with the demands of our busier lives as restrictions were lifted and some semblance of 'normality' returned. On the plus side, as co-authors we spent less time on Zoom calls and a little more time together, as we navigated our way through Matthew's Gospel. Our journey was all the richer for it.

The resource that is now in your hand invites you, the reader, to come on that journey and to engage more deeply with the Word as presented by Matthew.

Matthew's Gospel was written for a people trying to find their way amid the chaos and complications of the real world. It contains one of the most famous passages of the Scriptures, the Beatitudes, in which Jesus instructs the crowds, 'Blessed are the merciful' (Mt 5:7). In Matthew's Jesus, the 'kingdom of heaven' is made present, the world is transformed, and mercy is both a gift from God and a treasure to aspire to. There are many layers to unwrap and reflect on as we dive into this Gospel and enter into the heart of Jesus' calling to a radical new way of life.

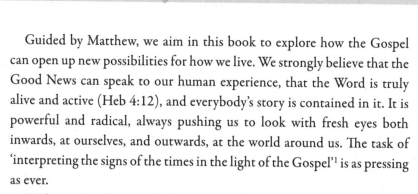

Guided by Matthew, we aim in this book to explore how the Gospel can open up new possibilities for how we live. We strongly believe that the Good News can speak to our human experience, that the Word is truly alive and active (Heb 4:12), and everybody's story is contained in it. It is powerful and radical, always pushing us to look with fresh eyes both inwards, at ourselves, and outwards, at the world around us. The task of 'interpreting the signs of the times in the light of the Gospel'[1] is as pressing as ever.

We hope that *The Deep End* will help readers to integrate faith and life by bringing them face to face with the Word of God. The message of Jesus, as presented by Matthew, has much to say to us. Our challenge is to see how this Word speaks to us each week so that we can respond to Jesus' invitation to love God, love our neighbour and live the Gospel with our lives.

How to Use This Book

The Church year begins on the First Sunday of Advent and moves through various seasons such as Christmas, Lent, Easter and Ordinary Time. Each year we focus on a particular Gospel for our Sunday liturgies and this follows a three-year cycle. We read and hear from the Gospel of Matthew on Sundays during Year A, Mark in Year B and Luke during Year C. Then, the cycle begins again. We also hear from John's Gospel during Lent, Easter and on some other feasts throughout the calendar.

And so, welcome to Year A, where you will read and hear from Matthew's Gospel throughout this liturgical year. The reflections in this book are designed as a companion for all those who would like to take a deeper look at the Sunday readings and to explore how the Gospel is relevant for our world today. The reflections are short and accessible and can easily be read as preparation for the Sunday liturgy, for personal reflection, or in a group. We also keep in mind all those who work in pastoral ministry, who may wish to draw on these reflections for use in various settings.

Each reflection includes the scripture reference for the gospel of the day. During Year A, these are mostly taken from Matthew's Gospel (with a few exceptions). We would highly recommend taking time to read the gospel text before the Sunday liturgy (see note on *Lectio Divina* below). So, having prepared, when we come to listen to the readings on Sunday, we hear the Word in a very different way, bringing fresh insights and experiences with us. The reflections in this book could also be revisited during a quiet period later in the week.

This is followed by a 'Go Deeper' section, which suggests some steps we might take to live out the gospel of the day more fully in our daily lives. As a companion to this book, we recommend that readers keep a journal where they can jot down any thoughts that arise for them and their responses to the 'Go Deeper' questions. It is our hope that by the end of the liturgical year, readers will feel they have been on a journey with the Jesus of Matthew's Gospel and will be able to look back and see the fruits of this journey.

'May the Word of God sown in the soil of our hearts, lead us in turn to sow hope through closeness to others. Just as God has done with us' (Pope Francis).[3]

Lectio Divina

Lectio Divina means *Sacred Reading*. With roots that go into the Old Testament, *Lectio* is one of the most ancient ways of listening for and hearing God's word in the Christian tradition. Thomas Keating notes that *Lectio* has been the mainstay of Christian monastic practice from the early days and consists of 'listening to the texts of the Bible as if one were in conversation with God and God were suggesting the topics for discussion'.[4] It is a personal encounter with God. It is not the intention of this book to replace this ancient spiritual practice of *Lectio Divina*. We encourage you to use *Lectio* as a method of reading the texts that are proposed for each Sunday, either in a group or in personal reflection. Then, you can move into *The Deep End* reflections for the day. They are food for the journey, not a substitute for time spent with God's Word. By setting aside some time each day, the fruits of this practice will grow throughout the week and across the year.

Much has been written about *Lectio Divina*, but we recommend the following method:

- *Lectio (Reading)*: We *read* the text two or three times, not with the head but with the heart. We linger on the words. We savour them. We gaze at the text, allowing ourselves to become familiar with it, allowing the Word to take root in us. What have we noticed? A word or phrase may have arisen. We repeat this word or phrase silently, like a mantra. In a group setting, people can be invited to speak this word aloud, without commenting on it.

- *Meditatio (Reflecting)*: This involves pondering or *reflecting* on the Word. What light does what we are hearing cast on what is *already* occurring in our lives, in our relationships, in all of our challenges and joys? What light does the Word cast on what is happening in our world or in Creation?

- *Oratio (Prayer)*: We may be moved in our hearts to respond through spontaneous *prayer*. This is our response to what we have read and heard. This prayer flows spontaneously from our reflection. As our prayer deepens, we begin to *rest* in God. The challenge for us is allowing space for this to happen, to discover the courage to let God speak in the silence, in the depths of our heart. It is a gift.

As we begin any spiritual practice, resistance can come in many forms like apathy or busyness. We recommend taking into careful consideration your preparation for this discipline. For example, find a quiet place, set aside a specific time of the day, turn off your phone and light a candle. Begin with mindful breaths, inhaling the peace of Christ and slowly exhaling any tension from the body. Do this a few times. Be aware of Christ's presence. Then begin your *Lectio*.

Through this ancient practice of *Lectio Divina*, we grow in awareness of Jesus alive in our hearts. We may feel an inner impulse to live out Christ's teachings in the world. In order to break open the Word even further, turn now to *The Deep End* reflections.

Matthew Who?

Matthew's Gospel is known as the 'First Gospel' not because it was the first to be written, but because it comes first in the New Testament. For many centuries it was thought of as the preferred Gospel of the Christian Church. So what do we know about Matthew, our gospel writer for this year? It is estimated that this Gospel was written sometime between AD 80 and 90 by a Greek-speaking, Jewish-Christian author.[5] Traditionally the author was thought to be Matthew the tax collector, who became a disciple of Jesus (Mt 9:9; 10:3). However, it is very unlikely that the author of this Gospel was a contemporary of Jesus.[6] So who did write 'Matthew'? We don't know; one possibility is that this anonymous author emerges from a community whose lineage goes back to the Jesus movement and who had links to Matthew the apostle.

Matthew's Gospel is likely to have been written in Antioch in Syria[7] for a community of Jewish-Christians whose membership was expanding to include a number of Gentile (non-Jewish) converts. Amongst this community were refugees of the First Jewish–Roman War (AD 66–70). In AD 70, the Romans destroyed the city of Jerusalem and its holy Temple in response to the Jewish revolt[8]. The Jerusalem Temple was the holiest place in the world for the Jewish people, a place where God was considered especially present. Its destruction was unfathomable. Now, with the Temple unlikely to be rebuilt and with the holy city resting in Roman hands, there were questions around what future lay ahead for Judaism. Matthew's Gospel was one response to this situation and provides 'insight into the early stages of the parting of the ways between Judaism and Christianity'.[9] The destruction of the Temple has a huge influence on Matthew's writing, as he seeks to show continuity between the ancient Jewish traditions, the Scriptures and the new Christian movement that had emerged.

Matthew had two main sources for his Gospel: Mark's Gospel (AD 70) and the source known as 'Q', which is thought to have contained the sayings of Jesus. Q was used as a source by Luke and Matthew but has been lost. There are also texts that are unique to Matthew, and these are sometimes known as 'M' material.[10] While Matthew draws on different sources, he gets creative with the material, freely rearranging it and adding his own theological perspective. The result is a complete literary work, which we will be delving into throughout this liturgical year.

What's Matthew's Story?

The gospel writers offer us four different lenses through which to look at the Jesus story. Although they have different audiences, styles and focuses, the hero of the story is the same, Jesus of Nazareth.

In Matthew's case, he is writing for a community at a crossroads. They are in exile and desiring direction for the future. In his writing, Matthew wishes to remain rooted in the Hebrew Scriptures (the Old Testament) and loyal to Jewish traditions. We see this in the opening genealogy of the Gospel, where Jesus' ancestry is traced back to Abraham (1:1–17). Throughout Jesus' life, from his childhood and all throughout his ministry, his teachings are seen as *fulfilment* of the promises that were made by God to the Jewish people. Fourteen times in this Gospel we read a variation of 'this was to fulfil what had been spoken by the Lord through the prophet'.[11] Matthew's Jesus continuously refers back to the Jewish Torah, the five books of the Law contained in the Hebrew Scriptures (5:17–20). But there was conflict within Judaism at this time, with many diverse groups holding different views but still very much under the banner of Judaism.

In addition, large numbers of Gentiles (non-Jews) were joining this Christian community in Syria, in keeping with the mission and ministry of Jesus:

'Go therefore and make disciples of all nations' (Mt 28:19). This was also creating tensions in the community for whom Matthew was writing, who wished to hold fast to their Jewish roots while embracing Jesus as the Messiah and their teacher. Matthew's Gospel attempts to provide navigation through this time of upheaval and transition for the community. 'These Jewish Christians saw their faith in Jesus as the Messiah and Son of God not as a rejection of their Jewish heritage but as the God-intended fulfilment of it... "Do not think I have come to abolish the law or the prophets; I have come not to abolish but to fulfil" (5:17).'[12] The Jesus movement was a renewal movement within Judaism; neither Jesus nor Matthew intended to start a new religion.[13]

Jesus in Matthew's Gospel is presented very much as the Messiah, the 'Son of God' (1:18, 20), 'Emmanuel', God-with-us (1:23), the incarnation of divine presence in the world. Jesus is a teacher and healer who is on a mission from beginning to end, but Jesus is not the Messiah that people expect. He is unconcerned with a political takeover, focusing more on shepherding the people with care and concern (2:6), especially the scattered and the lost (9:36; 10:6). Jesus ministers at the margins, to tax collectors and sinners, to the sick, those considered 'unclean', Gentiles, women and children. In Matthew's account of Jesus' ministry, the rules of exclusion are ignored and boundaries are crossed. It is not the 'wise and intelligent' (11:25–30) who are considered the greatest, but the 'children' and 'little ones' (18:1–7) who are put centre stage.

Matthew's Concerns

In Mark and Luke, the phrase 'kingdom of God' is used to describe the 'reign' of God on earth. Matthew, however, uses the phrase 'kingdom of heaven' to describe this concept, honouring the Jewish custom of not saying the name of the Divine, which is considered too holy to speak. This 'kingdom of heaven' is elusive, which is why Jesus used parables, stories and images to help explain what it means (Mt 13). The kingdom is a 'treasure' to be found. It is something hidden yet all powerful, offering renewed relationship with God and with one another, cultivating restoration and wholeness for all. Several of the 'kingdom' parables are unique to Matthew, including the parable of the treasure (13:44–51); the kingdom of heaven is so precious that its discovery requires us to put aside everything else and to live the kingdom values of humility, openness and compassion. The kingdom of heaven is not something that refers solely to the afterlife, but is rather a state of being or consciousness, something to be attained in the here and now but at the same time is not yet fulfilled.[14]

In order to enter this kingdom of heaven here on earth, Matthew's Jesus teaches that we must adopt certain attitudes and ways of being in this world, and there can be no half-measures. It's all or nothing. It is through the beautiful teaching of the Beatitudes and the famous Sermon on the Mount (chapters 5–7) that we read and hear what this kingdom looks like. The kingdom belongs to 'the poor in spirit', the 'peacemakers', those who are 'persecuted'. Followers of Jesus are expected to pass on mercy and forgiveness to others, resolve disputes and set their minds on modelling Jesus' way. It's in the famous Sermon on the Mount that we also hear the challenging call to love our enemies.

While Matthew might not go as far as Luke in his inclusion of women in the Jesus community, the involvement of women in the life and ministry of Jesus cannot be discounted. Given the social realities for women in a patriarchal society, Matthew's inclusion of women as exemplars in faith and discipleship is quite remarkable: for example, the inclusion of women's names in the opening genealogy (Mt 1:1–17), Jesus' encounter with the woman with the haemorrhage (9:20–22), the astounding encounter with the Canaanite Woman (15:21–28), the unnamed woman who anoints Jesus for burial in a gesture of loving service (26:6–13), the women who follow Jesus from Galilee and provide for him (27:55–56). It is the female followers of Jesus who stand with him at the hour of crucifixion, who attend to the burial and watch over the tomb; they are the first to witness and to proclaim the resurrection of Jesus to the world. It is the women who exemplify faith and discipleship.

By the end of Matthew's Gospel, we will see the mission of the Jesus community move outward to the Gentiles (non-Jews). The journey of

Matthew's Gospel is one that is moving outward, moving beyond the Roman Empire, beyond the Twelve, beyond patriarchy.

Matthew's Gospel has much to say to us today. It was written in a time when there was a lot of conflict in the Church community: there were insiders and outsiders, people mistrusted their religious and political leaders and ordinary people had no voice. Matthew presents Jesus ministering at the margins, overturning expectations about who is 'first' and who is 'last', and widening the circle of community to include 'all the nations'. 'It is a communal movement, a communal story constructed by communities of women and men and shaped by later communities of reception who heard it as their story also.'[15]

❧ 2 ❧

Advent

Introduction to Advent

Welcome to the first season of the Church's year, Advent. In the Christian calendar, Advent covers roughly the four weeks before Christmas, starting in late November or early December. Advent, however, is not simply a countdown to Christmas. Rather, we might think of this season as a signpost, marking our path, lighting our way, pointing to something beyond itself. Yes, it is a time of preparation for our celebration of the birth of Jesus, but it also marks a new Church year and a time to start over in our relationship with God and with others.

During the next few weeks, we will meet John the Baptist preparing the way for Jesus. We will meet Mary as she looks ahead to the birth of her baby and Elizabeth as she welcomes and celebrates this amazing news. In many ways, these characters are an unlikely bunch – a marginalised, pregnant young woman; an older woman unexpectedly pregnant, and an eccentric wilderness preacher – but we read that they are all 'filled with the Holy Spirit'. They are the first witnesses to Jesus' coming into the world, and we follow their stories as they announce him to others.

During Advent, we are invited to a real encounter with Jesus. It is a time to wake up and to rediscover our joy in life. It is a time to practise the words of Mary, 'Let it be', and to be open to what adventures may come our way. We become more aware of God's presence in the hidden places of our world, in ourselves and in the people around us. Can we be signposts lighting the path for others? At this busy time of year, we are often caught up in the frantic joys, and sometimes struggles, of the season. The lead-up to Christmas evokes different emotions and memories for each of us. As we enter this new season and new Church year, it is important to take some time to check in with ourselves. The gospel texts for the next few Sundays offer us the opportunity to go back to the beginning and enter fully into these Spirit-filled days when the advent of Jesus, the light of the world, is so eagerly anticipated.

First Sunday of Advent

Matthew 24:37–44

Keep awake

The 2007 film *The Bucket List* stars Morgan Freeman and Jack Nicholson as two terminally ill men who put together a wishlist of things to do before they 'kick the bucket'. They do a skydive, get tattoos and visit the pyramids. Some of the items on the list are more abstract: witness something truly majestic, help a total stranger for the good, find the joy in life. Of course we would live very differently if we *knew* our days were numbered. Sometimes it is only when the fragility of life is laid bare that we manage to get our priorities in order. Everything can change in an instant, with a phone call, an accident, the death of someone we love. These are the moments that stop us in our tracks. They come unexpectedly, like a thief in the night.

As we begin Advent, a season of joy and expectation, this might seem like a gloomy gospel to reflect on. Its tone is apocalyptic, but when Matthew was writing his Gospel, his community had these questions at the forefront of their minds: When will Jesus return? What signs will there be? Why is it taking so long? Jesus does not offer an answer to this question except to say, '*Keep awake*!' Instead of worrying about questions that we cannot possibly know the answer to, we might remember that what is important is how we are living now, today, in the present moment. Are we living aware of Christ present here and now in each person and in all of creation? Awakening to this miracle of universal love is a second coming or re-awakening we can get on board with. Advent is a very special time, a liminal space where we are full of expectant hope. It is an opportunity to take stock and *see* what is truly important; then we can experience the true joy which the season offers. Today's gospel invites us to be ready, not on tenterhooks and full of anxiety, but to be attentive, with open hearts, so that God's grace and love can enter once more this Christmas.

> ❝ God's hope for history seems to be that humanity will one day be able to recognize its own dignity as the divine dwelling place, which it also shares with the rest of creation.
>
> – Richard Rohr[16]

Go Deeper

- Advent is often experienced as an in-between space. Can you relate to periods of time like this in your own life? What is it like waiting on the threshold between old and new?

- Today's gospel urges us to *keep awake*! This Advent, how might you embrace this call, to live with greater awareness, waiting and watching for Christ's presence in the world around you?

Second Sunday of Advent

Matthew 3:1–12

Change is coming

John the Baptist was someone who lived on the edge of society but who carried a message for all. He lived simply, wearing 'camel's hair... and his food was locusts and wild honey'.[17] At some point in his life, John decided to break with the traditional religious system of his time and go wild! John goes into the desert, where he must ultimately deal with himself and with God who dwells within. He had an inner freedom that enabled him to live out this call to be a prophet, and when the religious leaders arrive at the River Jordan, John is not afraid to speak truth to power. He questions the fruits they have produced. While this 'brood of vipers' might have come to see what John is up to, the text says that they too came to be baptised by John. Perhaps they also longed for change. Considering the crowd that has arrived and the conflict that ensues with the authorities, we get a picture of a spiritual crisis in the community.

It is not by chance that we meet John the Baptist and his challenging message during Advent. His call to repent might not excite us, as we're in more of a celebratory mood these weeks, but 'to repent' literally means 'to turn around' or 'to return' (*metanoia*). It does not mean we riddle ourselves with guilt, rather it is an invitation to transformation, to turn away from what is not life-giving for us and embrace that which helps us to live a full, more balanced life. In this way, we create space to welcome Christ's grace and love at Christmas, and we become aware once more of his loving presence in our hearts and in the world around us. This is liberating and enables us to commit to love and the birthing of God in our hearts. How we prepare in these weeks is important and can lead to many blessings. Today John invites the people who have gathered, and us, to a change of heart.

"Christian life is a commitment to love, to give birth to God in one's own life and to become midwives of divinity in this evolving cosmos. We are to be wholemakers of love in a world of change.

– Ilia Delio[18]

Go Deeper

🐚 The Scriptures tell us of many challenging prophets like John. Who in our world today would we describe in a similar way? What are these prophets saying to us as a society? Are we hearing them?

🐚 John invites us to declutter our lives and make room for new possibilities. This Advent, what do you hope for? Can you create space for new possibilities, for a new birthing of God in your own life and in the world around you?

Feast of the Immaculate Conception

Luke 1:26–38

Blessed and brave

'Greetings, favoured one! The Lord is with you.' The greeting of the angel Gabriel to Mary is both startling and reassuring. It's a message from God, but what can it mean? She is 'perplexed' by the greeting of the angel who addresses her as 'favoured one' – an indication that God has been with her from the very first moment of her existence, that she is indeed blessed. Now she is to be the bearer of an even bigger blessing.

It's good news! But that doesn't take away from its shocking nature. Mary questions the angel, 'How can this be?' She must be thinking also of the ramifications: What will my family say? How will Joseph react? Will I be condemned? In Mary's world, being found to be pregnant outside of marriage could bring severe punishment, even the death penalty. It's a hugely precarious situation for a young girl to find herself in. We remember today all the young girls and women who have endured condemnation and exclusion after becoming pregnant or giving birth outside of the accepted societal and religious norms. We think of those who were 'sent away' to institutions and whose babies were taken from them without their consent. We remember all mothers who continue to face mistreatment and distress related to pregnancy and childbirth.

Mary, God's favoured one, knows the fear and uncertainty of carrying a baby and giving birth in an unsafe situation. But it is through this reality, that of a 'favoured' yet vulnerable young Jewish woman, that God chooses to enter our world, to make God's home. Mary's 'yes' to God's favour is brave and trusting. 'Here am I', she offers. This Advent, we invite God into our deepest fears and vulnerabilities. We do not make the journey alone; God is with us every step of the way.

"Mary, you see, could withstand and confront every standard of her synagogue and of her society, and take the poverty and the oppression and the pain to which that led because the will of God meant more to her than the laws of any system. That's the kind of woman God chose to do God's work.

– Joan Chittister[19]

Go Deeper

- Mary's 'yes' to God's plan wasn't easy. Her questioning and reflective nature were part of the process. Think of a time when you struggled to find your way. What helped you or brought you peace on your journey?

- 'Here am I.' Make these powerful words of Mary your prayer today. Let them guide you into God's presence.

Third Sunday of Advent

Matthew 11:2–11

What sort of Messiah is this?

John the Baptist is in prison because he challenged Herod for marrying his brother's wife. We learn later in the gospel that Herod has John beheaded.[20] While John is in prison, fear and doubt have set in. John is wondering if Jesus really is the Messiah. This is quite a turnaround from the John who felt unworthy to baptise Jesus in the Jordan and who declared 'the kingdom of heaven has come near' (3:2). John led quite an ascetic life and fasted frequently. The reports he now hears about Jesus include feasting, telling his disciples they do not have to fast, associating with tax collectors, drunkards and sinners. So one can understand why John began to have doubts. What sort of Messiah is this?

During these times, people had a checklist of ways to recognise the Messiah; it included liberating captives, healing the sick, raising the dead and restoring sight to the blind. Jesus' response to John's enquiries is that his actions speak for themselves. Jesus' actions are reminiscent of the Jubilee Year of Restoration (Lev 25; Isa 61) where injustices would be overturned, the land would be restored and the people given a fresh start. All of these things are being fulfilled in Jesus' ministry. The gospel ends with a paradox: John is the greatest that has ever been born; yet the people who are considered the 'lowest' or the 'least' in this world are considered even greater than John by God. The more we reflect on this statement, the more we come to see that both aspects of it are true and in harmony with one another. In this new age that John has announced, the poorest and those considered the lowest in society will be greater than John himself. This is the kingdom of heaven that Matthew announces to his readers. A new era, a great upheaval has begun.

"The problem is not feeding the poor, or clothing the naked, or visiting the sick, but rather recognising that the poor, the naked, the sick, prisoners, and the homeless have the dignity to sit at our table, to feel 'at home' among us, to feel part of a family. This is a sign that the Kingdom of Heaven is in our midst.

– Pope Francis[21]

Go Deeper

- John has doubts in today's gospel and that's ok. Doubt is not the enemy. It demands to be expressed and explored and offers an opportunity for greater insight and deeper understanding. When have you known this to be true?

- Jesus' ministry brings restoration to people who are captive, healing to the sick, people set free. Where do we see this in-breaking kingdom of heaven in our society today? Who are the prophets bringing it about?

Fourth Sunday of Advent

Matthew 1:18–24

The dream

Today's gospel recalls the central role played by Joseph in the story of Jesus. While Matthew's Gospel is very clearly an account of Jesus 'the Messiah, the son of David, the son of Abraham', Joseph takes centre stage in the first scene of the Jesus story. He is introduced as a good man with a serious dilemma. Instead of publicly calling off his engagement to Mary – leaving her to face severe punishment or even the death penalty – he opts to 'dismiss her quietly'. This incident introduces a tension that will be seen throughout Matthew's Gospel between obedience to the letter of the law and 'righteousness'.

There is more to the story. In a dream, Joseph receives a message about the baby, whose name is given as Jesus.[22] Matthew adds a note here that this fulfils the prophecy of the birth of *Emmanuel*, 'God is with us'. God is present – God-with-us – from the earliest moments of Jesus' story. Joseph's response is immediate and radical. Rather than doing what's expected, or even taking the kinder option available to him, he follows the invitation of God and forges a new path. This new way is very much in the spirit of the later teachings of Jesus, particularly when he counsels his followers, 'You have heard that it was said ... but I say to you ... ' (5:21–48). Joseph is open and compassionate, going above and beyond for the sake of the kingdom.

Joseph is sometimes depicted in statue form as 'Sleeping Joseph'. He shows us how God reveals God's plan in times of silence and rest. Even when we are doing the right things and living a virtuous life, God can surprise us, picking apart the lines we draw between people. We are constantly being nudged out of our comfort zone, towards others, to become ever more compassionate, loving and open to God's dream for us.

" Only in the sacredness of inward silence does the soul truly meet the secret, hiding God. The strength of resolve, which afterward shapes life, and mixes itself with action, is the fruit of those sacred, solitary moments. There is a divine depth in silence. We meet God alone.

– Frederick William Robertson[23]

Go Deeper

The Bible has many examples of God speaking to people through their dreams.[24] Do you pay attention to your dreams, keep a journal or pray about them? Perhaps they could be viewed as a gift or an invitation, bringing new insight or spiritual energy.

❧ 3 ❧

Christmas

Introduction to the Season of Christmas

In the liturgical calendar, the season of Christmas runs from midnight (or nightfall) of 24 December and continues until the Feast of the Baptism of Jesus. During these Christmas weeks, those of us living in the northern hemisphere tend to hibernate. The earth has tilted away from the sun and, even though the winter solstice has passed on 21 December, the days are still dark and quiet, the soil resting, and our attention is drawn inwards. Many people find winter difficult; indeed, with very little sunlight and the weather cold, it can be a tough time. But it is during these weeks that Christians celebrate something amazing: God entering into humanity, putting on skin and living among us as a full human person, in a way that we still find hard to put into words. Jesus – a Palestinian Jew, who was born into a homeless family in an animal shelter in a remote part of the Roman Empire – is marginalised from the very beginning. Yet he is someone who transformed history and who continues to transform our lives today.

Into all the harrowing struggles of our world, then and now, God is born. This is what these Christmas days invite us to contemplate and celebrate. Christ is born again each year in our hearts, if we can make room for him there, and in our world, if we look with awareness in ordinary places. As

we light the white candle on the Advent wreath on Christmas morning, let us remember what it represents: the peace, unity and hope for which the world desperately longs. Matthew invites us to rejoice with the angels and the shepherds, joining together in praise, singing, 'Glory to God in the highest heaven and on earth peace, goodwill among people.' Matthew invites us to journey with the holy family as they flee Bethlehem and become refugees in Egypt, and John brings us into the beautiful mystery of God dwelling in the material universe. There is much to ponder.

A note on the texts for Christmas Day: in the lectionary, there are three different gospels that may be read on Christmas Day. At 'midnight' Mass – even if it takes place before midnight – we hear the account of Jesus' birth, including the message to the shepherds (Lk 2:1–14). For those up bright and early on Christmas Morning, at the Dawn Mass we read about the visit of the shepherds to Bethlehem (Lk 2:15–20). The gospel reading for the Mass later in the day is taken from John's Gospel (Jn 1:1–18). Since this reading is also used on the Second Sunday after Christmas, you will find a reflection for it on page 42.

Christmas Midnight Mass

Luke 2:1–14

Hidden in the ordinary

Tonight we celebrate the joy of Jesus' birth as told to us by Luke, where God enters into a truly complex situation.

A census has been called. In those times a census was not taken for the well-being of the people but to take count of the assets of the country, its wealth, animals and crops. This information was then used to exploit the people, to instil fear and impose taxes; it was a further act of oppression by a foreign power. It does not matter that Mary is heavily pregnant, she and her family must travel to Joseph's ancestral home, Bethlehem.

Luke only gives one sentence to the actual birth of Jesus, and you'd nearly miss it. He then focuses his attention on the shepherds. There is a reason for their presence. Shepherds were considered social outcasts because of their close contact with animals. Their lives would have been full of poverty, fear and struggle. This scene that Luke paints is not tranquil. This is a subversive setting, on the margins. It is into this mess that God comes as a homeless child. We are being invited to expect the unexpected as the scene is set for the world to be turned upside down in solidarity with the marginalised; it is in their name that the shepherds are chosen. The angels rejoice with the shepherds, the 'highest' and the 'lowest', giving glory to God together.

As you sing the 'Gloria' during this Christmas season, come back to this marginal space where it was first sung, with the angels and the shepherds in a field on the edge of Empire. Tonight's gospel shows us that God reveals God-self in the most unexpected places: in a field rather than a temple, in a feeding trough rather than a palace. God does not abandon us to the brokenness of this world, rather God's promise is one of liberation and deep peace for all. It is for this reason we rejoice. *Shalom. Síochán.*

"Do not be dismayed by the brokenness of the world. All things break. And all things can be mended. Not with time, as they say, but with intention. So go. Love intentionally, extravagantly, unconditionally. The broken world waits in darkness for the light that is you.

– L. R. Knost[25]

Go Deeper

- Can you recall an experience of finding God hidden in the ordinary? Look back over your day. Where were the moments of light, joy or blessing?

- Jesus was born into a country experiencing oppression by a brutal, foreign power. Where in our world experiences similar oppression today? Who longs for liberation, freedom and peace? Pray that peace is born in all those places and within our own hearts this Christmas.

Christmas Dawn Mass

Luke 2:15–20

Time to ponder

We pick up today where Luke's Gospel left off last night, following the story of the shepherds as they proceed to Bethlehem. Their excitement is evident – 'Let us go now' – and they proceed with haste. The scene that greets them couldn't be simpler: Mary, Joseph and a baby lying in the manger, as the angel had predicted. Their delight is contagious, 'all who heard it were amazed at what the shepherds told them'. In an echo of the heavenly host, they return to their lives glorifying and praising God. In the midst of this joyful story, we can easily find ourselves glossing over one short sentence about Mary, who 'treasured all these words and pondered them in her heart'. Her reaction is almost the opposite to that of the shepherds – where they are exuberant, she is pensive; where they outwardly share the news, Mary's focus is inward as she ponders the unfolding mystery.

As we celebrate Christmas, we are asked to open up our hearts, to make our hearts a crib, a place to welcome and encounter Jesus. What does this mean? As we hear the Christmas story today, what effect does it have on us? Perhaps we are like the shepherds, bubbling over with joy. We might identify with Mary, still trying to figure out what it all means. There is room for both. There is a depth and intimacy to Mary's understanding of Jesus, whereas the shepherds have perhaps only scratched the surface. Our faith and our relationship with God go through seasons. The ups and downs of life can take us by surprise, and we might find ourselves looking at things in a different way. When the flurry of Advent is over, Christmas has a way of stopping us in our tracks, giving us time to rest in wonderment and give thanks for God's faithfulness in our lives. This is a time to sit with Mary as she treasures and ponders.

❝ I am not alone at all, I thought. I was never alone at all. And that, of course, is the message of Christmas. We are never alone. Not when the night is darkest, the wind coldest, the world seemingly most indifferent. For this is still the time God chooses.

– Taylor Caldwell[26]

Go Deeper

- 'All who heard it were amazed.' When have you been amazed by words spoken to you? Who spoke? Did it spur an emotional reaction, a new insight? What is it saying to you now?

- The sense in this narrative is that God is faithful; this is why Mary ponders and the shepherds rejoice. Do you have a sense of God's faithfulness in your own life? Find space to sit quietly during these Christmas days to ponder this.

Sunday in the Octave of Christmas/ Feast of the Holy Family

Matthew 2:13–15, 19–23

Displaced

There are few details about Jesus' early years. In today's Gospel, Matthew offers an insight into some of the challenges faced by this young family. While Jesus is still small, Joseph is urged in a dream to escape to Egypt as Jesus' life is under threat. Herod's presence again casts a dark shadow, threatening their peace and very survival. And, as before, Joseph acts immediately. They flee under cover of darkness, leaving their home for another country, not knowing when, or if, it would be safe to return home.

Millions of people in our world today do not have to use their imagination to understand this experience – they are living it. Like Jesus' family, so many are forced to leave their home country due to persecution, war or climate change, entering a time of hardship and uncertainty. As Ishmael Beah describes in his memoir, 'One of the unsettling things about my journey, mentally, physically, and emotionally, was that I wasn't sure when or where it was going to end.'[27] Beah was twelve years old when he fled his village in Sierra Leone after it was attacked by rebels. Separated from his family, he was forced into the army as a child soldier and fought for three years before being rescued.

The precarious experience of displacement is at the heart of the experience of the child Jesus. When the family returns from Egypt, unsure whether the threat has passed, they flee again, eventually setting up home in Nazareth. It's a turbulent start to their family life. We remember today all displaced people living an unpredictable existence, travelling to reach safety, separated from friends and family, unsure where they will set up home. We reflect also on our responsibility to our sisters and brothers all over the world who are in need of welcome and refuge.

> **“** If all people are my brothers and sisters, and if the world truly belongs to everyone, then it matters little whether my neighbour was born in my country or elsewhere... [We] can offer a generous welcome to those in urgent need, or work to improve living conditions in their native lands by refusing to exploit those countries or to drain them of natural resources.
>
> – Pope Francis[28]

Go Deeper

- This passage prompts reflection on Joseph as he quietly takes care of his family. Who are the people in your family or friendship circles who quietly keep you going?

- Compassion for vulnerable strangers was a key element of Jesus' ministry, regardless of their nationality or social status. As his followers, we are called to offer welcome and hospitality to those in need. How does your community reach out to migrants, asylum seekers and refugees?

Second Sunday of Christmas

John 1:1–18

He came to what was his own

Thanks to modern science, we have learned more about our universe in the past fifty years than ever before. We are the first generations to know that the observable universe is 13.8 billion years old and that this universe continues to evolve and expand. Planet Earth, our common home, is 4.6 billion years old, orbiting a sun that is one of trillions of stars in our galaxy. Our galaxy, the Milky Way, is one of billions of galaxies in this expanding universe. Astrophysicists tell us that our universe began life as a tiny speck that has unfolded over billions of years to form galaxies, planets, flowers, music, and you and me. Everything is connected in this New Universe Story.[29] While we might assume that this story is in conflict with our faith, nothing could be further from the truth. For as science discovers the how, the great faiths and spiritualities of the world contemplate that which gives life meaning and purpose.

The opening words of St John's Gospel help us to meditate on this great mystery as John contemplates the Source of all things: 'In the beginning was the Word...' in Greek, *Logos*. This *Logos* (Word) has far more meaning than its English translation can give. It refers to the Divine, Creator God, Mother and Father of all things, Wisdom, that which is forever. John tells us that not one thing came to be without God, who was the cause of that moment of creation when our universe began. From this event, all else evolved into being: the stars, the Earth, our vast ecosystems, billions of species, all the people who have ever lived. We read that 'the Word', Christ, 'was in the beginning with God ... and without him not one thing came into being'.

Every year at Christmas we celebrate God reaching down into humanity, but we also celebrate God's continuing presence in our lives and in our world today, fully at work in creation at every stage, then, now and forever. For creation and incarnation are not different events, but the same event, ongoing. Do we see this glory?

> **God is always incarnate, always bound to the world as its lover, as close to it, as we are to our own bodies, and concerned before all else to see that the body, God's world, flourishes.**
>
> **– Sallie McFague[30]**

Go Deeper

- John writes that from Christ's fullness we have all received grace upon grace. With gratitude, reflect on these words this week. Where do you see Christ's grace in your own life and in the world around you, in nature, in other people?

- This week, sit with these beautiful words from the prologue of John's Gospel, savouring them and letting them rest in your heart.

Epiphany

Matthew 2:1–12

By another road

The visit of the wise men from 'the East' marks a key moment when Christ's light shines out to all nations. Typical of Matthew's Gospel, the good news moves from Jesus outwards, in a ripple effect. The inclusion of the Gentiles in the community of faith, from the very beginning of Jesus' life, would have been significant to the early readers of Matthew's Gospel, a Jewish-Christian community who were at a crossroads and discerning whether to embrace the Gentile mission. The word 'epiphany' comes from the Greek *epiphainen*, which means to shine upon or make known, to illuminate. Imagine the light the magi carried in their hearts after that encounter.

There's another element to this story. The threat posed by the tyrant king Herod casts a dark shadow over the cosy glow of the visit of the wise men. Herod asks the magi to report back to him with the location of the newborn Messiah. They 'hear' the king but happily, they decide to defy the unjust order and return home 'by another road'. We might call it an act of civil disobedience. This gospel encourages us to think beyond our boundaries, in more ways than one. When we find our treasure, like the wise men did, it changes us, and we set out on a new path, perhaps more difficult but faithful to our truth.

We think today of all those who fight for justice in the face of pressure. One example is a congregation of women religious who were part of a campaign in Pennsylvania opposing the construction of a natural gas pipeline. The Sisters, whose mission involves honouring the sacredness of creation and preserving the earth for current and future generations, built an outdoor chapel in a corn-field, on the proposed path of the pipeline. The chapel drew people of all faiths to prayer and reflection about the use of land and other natural resources. These wise women saw the light and found a new way to shine it out into the world.

" **Epiphany is about revelation, the kind of sudden brightness that lights up the landscape of a mind or a community or a whole social order. The light reveals, but not passively; it summons and sends.**

– Bill Wylie-Kellermann[31]

Go Deeper

🐌 Recall an 'epiphany' moment in your life, when you felt a light dawning, or you received new insight. How did it change you or set you on a new path?

🐌 We bring to mind all those who stand up for what is right, who challenge the powerful. At the beginning of a new year, we might consider how we could support such efforts.

The Baptism of Jesus

Matthew 3:13–17

The Great Turning

Full of conviction, passion and righteous anger, John the Baptist pleads with people to turn around and 'prepare the way' (3:3). Yet, in today's gospel we meet a different John. He is surprised to see that Jesus has arrived to be baptised by him and feels unworthy of such a task. Jesus explains to John that this is a necessary signal at the beginning of his ministry, a public statement of identity. It is also more than that. In Jesus' first spoken words in Matthew's Gospel he says this baptism is 'to fulfil all righteousness', and here we have the central theme of Matthew's Gospel announced. In the Old Testament, 'righteousness' literally means right relationship. It is not solely focused on an individual's repentance but refers to the turning around of God's people, a collective turning, towards restoration and justice across the land. Jesus at the Jordan stands with God's people, in solidarity yes, but also in his full human experience, in his living, suffering, dying, and in the making of straighter paths. Jesus is baptised in the Jordan, because he is modelling the way for humanity as we strive for 'righteousness' in our communities and in the complexities that life brings for each of us.

We are not short of situations in our world which require people to *turn around* and walk a new path. The environmental crisis is one example, calling the entire human species to wake up and walk an entirely different path in order to ensure a sustainable future for all. This requires a *collective turning*, what authors Joanna Macy and Chris Johnson call '*The Great Turning*'.[32] They describe our current situation as one where we are living through three realities at once: '*Business as Usual*' (measuring progress by economic growth), '*The Great Unravelling*' (the destruction of our only home in order to achieve economic growth), and '*The Great Turning*'. This *Great Turning* is the global awakening, the ecological revolution that is underway and which must be fully embraced if we are to bring healing to our world.

> **" In the past, changing the self and changing the world were often regarded as separate endeavours and viewed in either-or terms. But in the story of the Great Turning, they are recognized as mutually reinforcing and essential to one another.**
>
> **– Joanna Macey & Chris Johnson.**[33]

Go Deeper

- John almost lets feelings of inadequacy prevent him from carrying out his vocation in life. Can you relate to this in your own life? Who came to encourage you? What lessons were learned?
- As individuals and as communities what do we need to turn away from? What do we need to turn up to? What do we need to turn towards?

♠ 4 ♠
Ordinary Time (1)
Introduction to Ordinary Time

When people hear the word 'ordinary' they immediately think of something plain, unremarkable, the opposite of extraordinary. We often tend to think of Ordinary Time as a sort of 'everything else' season – if it's not Advent, Christmas, Lent or Easter, it is Ordinary Time. Yet we should not dismiss this season or treat it as an anti-climax or downtime in between the big feasts. The term itself comes from the Latin *ordinalis* meaning ordered, so it simply refers to the way the Sundays are named in a numbered sequence. The rhythm of the liturgical seasons also reflects the cycle of life in the natural world and the rhythm of our own lives.

During Ordinary Time we hear the stories of Jesus' life and ministry through his teaching and parables, through his meals and healings, through his conversations with followers and challengers, right up to his final journey towards and into Jerusalem. Most of these accounts are of course taken from Matthew's Gospel this year, and in following them we get a real sense of journeying with Jesus and of his vision of the kingdom of heaven as a way of life in the here and now.

There is much richness to be discovered when we allow the story to unfold from one Sunday to the next. We are invited to be active participants in the gospel story, using it as a time to draw closer to Jesus and to grow and

mature in our understanding and faith. Don't let this anything-but-ordinary time pass you by.

While defined as one season in the Church calendar, Ordinary Time is broken into two different periods. The first of these (Ordinary Time 1) runs from the Baptism of the Lord to the start of Lent, and the second (Ordinary Time 2) from just after Pentecost right up to the first Sunday of Advent, when the new liturgical year starts again. Since the beginning of Lent varies from year to year, depending on the date of Easter, the number of weeks in Ordinary Time 1 and 2 will vary also. During Ordinary Time, we also celebrate a number of special Feast Days, which you will find highlighted in this book.

Second Sunday in Ordinary Time

John 1:29–34

Look, here he is

In today's gospel, John the Baptist is inviting us to *look* at Jesus. He calls Jesus the 'lamb of God who takes away the sins of the world'. We hear these words often in our liturgies and today we are invited to meditate on them more closely. In Jesus' time, two lambs were sacrificed in the Temple in Jerusalem each day. Lambs were also sacrificed if individuals needed to perform an act of ritual purity. John refers to Jesus as the lamb of God, because he knows that for Jesus living and preaching a love that was and still is radical for many will involve suffering, even death, at the hands of the systems that he challenges.

Sin is a word we are not fond of these days, and for good reason, but one definition of 'sin' is a 'broken relationship', between people and themselves, people and the world and between people and God. We are not short of situations in our world where this is reality: poverty, greed, violence, war, hunger, unjust economic systems, and even ecological sin. In 2019, at a Vatican conference on 'Criminal Justice and Corporate Business', Pope Francis stated that 'ecological sin' would be included in the Catechism of the Catholic Church. He said that ecological sin 'manifests itself in acts and habits of pollution and destruction of the harmony of the environment'. He included 'ecocide', the massive contamination of air, land and water resources, the wide scale destruction of biodiversity and 'any action capable of producing an ecological disaster or destroying an ecosystem.'[34]

The 'sins of the world' are all around us, but so are those who strive to 'take away' these sins. Jesus' immense love is not a passive love; he does not accept that sin and death will have the final say, yet he comes with the gentleness of a lamb. Todays' gospel invites us to look at the lamb of God, actively easing the world's suffering. When we hear these words, may we be reminded of all those who sacrifice much to ease the sufferings of others. This is Christ, the 'lamb of God' active and present in our here and now.

> "Love is reckless; not reason. Reason seeks a profit. Love comes on strong, consuming herself unabashed. Yet, in the midst of suffering, love proceeds like a millstone, hard-surfaced and straight forward. Having died to self-interest, she risks everything and asks for nothing. Love gambles away every gift God bestows.
>
> – Rumi[35]

Go Deeper

- Where do you notice 'ecological sin' in your community, in the world today?
- John the Baptist invites us to look, *'here is the lamb of God'*. Where do you see Jesus humbly and lovingly active in the world today?

Third Sunday in Ordinary Time

Matthew 4:12–23

Gathering

Jesus begins his ministry with the first of many 'gatherings'. Hearing that John has been arrested, he 'withdraws' to Galilee.[36] He is shaken and perhaps he too is under threat. Nevertheless, he preaches the same bold message as John: 'Repent, for the kingdom of heaven has come near.' This is the message the disciples will later be sent to preach (Mt 10:7). Matthew interprets Jesus' arrival in Galilee as fulfilment of the prophet Isaiah's declaration that a 'great light' would shine in the darkness. The reference to 'Galilee of the Gentiles'[37] offers a clue as to who will be gathered and included in Jesus' mission.

Fishing metaphors feature heavily throughout Matthew's Gospel. Jesus starts his ministry in the fishing village of Capernaum by gathering a crew of disciples – two sets of brothers, all fishermen. In terms of social status, fishermen were low down in the pecking order. Their occupation was precarious at best, leaving them economically vulnerable, and they had to pay taxes to the Roman Empire, which made them unpopular. They might seem an unlikely choice for a Messiah starting his mission. Simon (Peter) and Andrew are casting their net out when Jesus calls them, quipping 'Follow me, and I will make you fish for people.' Similarly, James and John abandon their net-mending 'immediately' to follow him. They are 'all in'. The mission has momentum; these fisherfolk are needed as the sea is ripe for fishing. Their task will be to draw others in, and the net will be cast indiscriminately, far and wide. Later, Jesus will compare the kingdom of heaven to a 'dragnet', catching fish of every kind (Mt 13:47).

When we join together for liturgy we often begin by acknowledging our 'gathering', indicating that we are being called out of our ordinary, everyday lives to gather as community, aware of God's presence among us. We are also called every day into God's service, invited to repentance, a change of heart.

Like the disciples, we are called, and we call; we are gathered, and we gather. When we are drawn in by Jesus, we extend the same open welcome to others. The kingdom is at hand, and Jesus' net gathers indiscriminately, regardless of social or economic status.

> **" How wonderful it is that nobody need wait a single moment before starting to improve the world.**
>
> **– Anne Frank[38]**

Go Deeper

- The fishing net is a powerful image, representing Jesus' invitation to all. How do we model this openness in our lives? Do we gather people in or cast them away?

- The first disciples are ordinary people called to an extraordinary mission. A life following Jesus involves taking risks. It is urgent, immediate and 'all in'. Reflect on this challenge for your life.

Fourth Sunday in Ordinary Time

Matthew 5:1–12

An alternate wisdom

Today we read and hear from the opening verses of Matthew's most famous passage, 'The Sermon on the Mount', and it is here that the good news of Jesus Christ unfolds. The Beatitudes are at the heart of Jesus' teachings, yet it is unfortunate that we hear so little about them. The Beatitudes are far from a box-tick exercise in order to receive God's love. On the contrary, they speak a language of grace. They do not condemn, rather they give us a glimpse of a life that is lived out of the call to love God and neighbour, spoken in a way that motivates rather than criticises. While the first part of each beatitude speaks about the present and is rooted in human experience, the second part invites us to contemplate what is to come. The Beatitudes are not idealising some future utopia either but are lived and experienced in the here and now. It sounds like a paradox or a riddle, but here we are lovingly invited to grow into what the beatitudes praise. This is what a real *metanoia* (a turning around) looks like. As the Sermon on the Mount unfolds, we are invited into whole relationships, with God, with our loved ones, even with our enemies! The Beatitudes are a predisposition for what follows. Like a compass, they orient us towards restoration. The first beatitude sets the scene for everything that follows:

'Blessed are the poor in spirit for theirs is the kingdom of heaven'.

This beatitude, ironically, praises spiritual poverty or emptiness and invites us to gently examine our inner attitude and attachments. Then we might be more open to receive God's grace into our hearts. The reward is not necessarily referring to the afterlife. The kingdom of heaven is a state of being that can be experienced in the here and now. The Beatitudes promise comfort, greater awareness and intimacy with God. Through the Beatitudes, Jesus blesses those that this world crushes: the meek, the peacemakers, those who are persecuted. The Beatitudes turn the world upside down with their dramatic reversals and are the essence of the in-breaking kingdom of heaven.

> **"Jesus embodied the highest level of enlightenment. He spent his brief adult life describing it, teaching it, and passing it onto future generations. Jesus intended to save the world by showing others the path to God-consciousness.**
>
> – Deepak Chopra[39]

Go Deeper

🐚 This week, spend time ruminating on one of the Beatitudes each day. See what arises. Who are the poor in spirit? Who are the peacemakers around you or those who are persecuted?

🐚 Living the Beatitudes in today's world involves living an alternative reality to the status quo. We are invited to dream and to take risks. What might this look like for you?

Fifth Sunday in Ordinary Time

Matthew 5:13–16

People of light

The hymn 'This Little Light of Mine' was written as a gospel song for children in the 1920s. It later became an anthem for the civil rights movement in the US in the 1960s. It's associated in particular with Fannie Lou Hamer, a civil rights activist who dedicated her life to the struggle for Black voting rights and against racial segregation and injustice. Hamer was threatened, arrested, beaten and shot at, yet was not deterred from her cause. Her most famous saying – 'I'm sick and tired of being sick and tired' – shone a light on the plight of the Black community. Hamer was a powerful singer whose favourite song was, 'This Little Light of Mine'.[40] The song came to signify hope in the fight for equal rights and freedom.

The lyrics are based on the Sermon on the Mount, in which Jesus instructs his disciples, 'You are the salt of the earth ... You are the light of the world.' The 'salt and light' sayings point outwards to their mission in the world. Salt must hold its taste in order to season, and a lamp must be lit in order to shine. Jesus is preparing the disciples to go out, to shine brightly and so to glorify God. What is this light? Some might call it the 'divine spark', God's presence in us. We recognise this light in the shining example of how one person or group can change the world. Without the efforts of Fannie Lou Hamer, Rosa Parkes, Martin Luther King Jr., and all who were part of the civil rights movement, our world would be a different place. These 'salt of the earth' people brought light to many. The fight for justice continues today in those who lift up their voices to ensure people are treated fairly. People of light sit with those in darkness, in pain or who are persecuted. They challenge unfair systems. It can be tempting for people of light to become disheartened. But they carry on, bringing about change, however slowly, shining light in the darkness.

“Sometimes it seems like to tell the truth today is to run the risk of being killed. But if I fall, I'll fall five feet four inches forward in the fight for freedom. I'm not backing off.

– Fannie Lou Hamer[41]

Go Deeper

🍃 You can hide your 'divine spark', or you can let it shine. Jesus calls all of us to be people of light. What in your life is blocking your light from shining out to others?

🍃 What salt does for food, Christians are called to do for the world. You might recall someone who brought 'taste' to your life, encouraging you on your journey, offering hope, a new insight. What was their legacy?

Sixth Sunday in Ordinary Time

Matthew 5:17–37

Love is the key

The Sermon on the Mount continues and today's gospel starts with Jesus' declaration that he has not come to 'abolish the law or the prophets' but to 'fulfil' them. This is an important theme for Matthew. It can be understood in different ways: Jesus is fulfilling, i.e. bringing about that which was promised by the prophets and the law, but also Jesus himself *is* the fulfilment. He reveals and is the true and deeper meaning of the law.[42] Later in the Gospel Jesus identifies love of God and of neighbour as the greatest commandments, saying 'On these two commandments hang all the law and the prophets' (Mt 22:40).

Today, we hear several teachings beginning with the formula, 'You have heard that it was said ... but I say to you ...'. Jesus is not contradicting the law but strengthening and intensifying it. Not only should we 'not murder' – as required by the law – but we are also to avoid anger and insults, which are placed on the same spectrum. Jesus is talking about more than our actions. When we explore this teaching in the context of love, it involves everything from our inner attitude to the way we interact with others, in small situations as well as big. Reconciliation and harmonious relationships are to take priority over worship. In another example, the commandment to 'not commit adultery' reaches beyond outward faithfulness to our inner thoughts, what's in our hearts. Jesus' talk of the tearing out of eyes and cutting off of limbs seems designed to shock his audience, and these words are doubly shocking to the modern listener. We may be familiar with the commandments and rules of a life of faith, but have we engraved them in our hearts? These teachings of Jesus illustrate what he means by 'righteousness'. If love is at the heart of the law, we will do more than simply obey but endeavour to act with compassion, respect and self-giving.

"True love is delicate and kind, full of gentle perception and understanding, full of beauty and grace, full of joy unutterable ... With such a love one would see all things new; we would begin to see people as they really are, as God sees them.

– Dorothy Day

Go Deeper

Emotions are a central part of our daily lives. Yet we can struggle to process 'negative' emotions or even learn to suppress them. Emotions are not good or bad, but our reactions to them can be positive or negative. What would it be like to experience emotions for what they are – as visitors, rather than our whole identity? Reflect on this in light of today's Gospel. Note Jesus' guidance on the potential for reconciliation and inner growth.

Seventh Sunday in Ordinary Time

Matthew 5:38–48

A love that liberates

This is one of the most challenging passages in the Gospels, sometimes described as Jesus' most unreasonable command. The instruction to love our enemies appears to contradict the calls for retribution we hear in the world around us and our instinct for self-preservation, but Jesus is not encouraging passiveness. He is inviting people to a 'third way': to make a nonviolent stand when faced with persecution. The easy option is to retaliate, to not see our sister or brother standing before us, but by offering the 'other cheek', we acknowledge our shared sacred humanity. 'Loving our enemies' is a call to constantly move towards restoring relationships.

Jesus reminds us that everyone is a child of God, that God loves everyone and every part of creation, without exception. It's easier said than done, but Jesus calls us to meet hatred with love, to make room for forgiveness. What happens to Jesus at the hands of his persecutors does not diminish his love for them. The exhortation to 'be perfect as your heavenly Father is perfect' is a deep call to love with the fierceness that God loves.

In 1987, just hours after his twenty-year-old daughter Marie was killed in an IRA bomb in Enniskillen, came the powerful words of Gordon Wilson, 'I bear no ill will. I bear no grudge. Dirty sort of talk is not going to bring her back to life. She's in heaven, and we shall meet again. I will pray for these men tonight and every night.' His words had a powerful impact on the Northern Ireland conflict. His extraordinary capacity to forgive the people who caused him pain helped the slow process of healing and reconciliation. Gordon Wilson was the personification of the words of Jesus to 'love your enemies and pray for those who persecute you'. That is a love that liberates.

❝ I can't wait for my neighbour to love me! If I do, the space between us may never be bridged. Mine must be a creative and often costly love, as is God's love of me ... There are [those] who don't love me at all, nor do I love them! And yet my little love-rope must be cast out to them: I must wish them well, and not demand a responding rope from their side of the divide.

– Brian Grogan[43]

Go Deeper

🐾 With so much war and conflict in the world, it is easy to become despondent. But in every situation, there are people striving for peaceful solutions. Can you recall any stories of hope amid conflict?

🐾 You might not consider yourself as having enemies, but what about people who have hurt you or with whom you've fallen out, or whom you struggle to love? Can you pray for them and wish them well?

In the past, Lent was often seen as a time to look down on ourselves. Words such as 'temptation', 'evil', 'sin' and 'guilt' were often dominant, leaving some people in darkness and despair. This was extremely damaging for many. Thankfully, today we are trying to let go of such language and see Lent for what it really is, a time for transformation and encounter. Indeed, for some people today, it is one of their favourite Church seasons! New Year's resolutions are probably well out the window by the time Lent comes around, so in a real sense it brings us the opportunity of a new beginning, a chance to start again. Lent offers us a time for deep reflection, and for those of us who hear and read the Gospel each week during this season, the texts offer a richness that can bring freshness to our lives. Lent is a journey of preparation for Easter, a time to refresh our relationship with God, with those we love and cherish, with those we find difficult to love and with God's creation. Lent is like a time of stocktaking: what's here that shouldn't be? What do I need to let go of? Where do I need to spend more time? The intention is not to beat ourselves up; rather, it is to set out on a journey that will help us live our best lives with our hearts open. This is what Jesus wants for us.

We read on the First Sunday of Lent that our first stop is the wilderness. Here we embrace three tools to assist us: prayer, fasting and almsgiving. A

suggestion for this season might be to spend more time with God's Word, to give up some luxury, and to either donate what you can to your favourite charity or give your time to something or someone. These practices help us to focus and to grow in deeper awareness of what it means to be a follower of Jesus.

During this time, it is good for us to remove ourselves from our normal routines, to be still, and to stop and breathe. We need not be afraid of this, for the Gospel shows us that time spent in the wilderness is Spirit-led, and we are not alone. We hope that you can use the following reflections to spend more time this Lent with God's Word, in prayer for transformation, renewal and encounter with the One who journeys with us.

First Sunday of Lent

Matthew 4:1–11

The challenge of indifference

We don't hear much about temptation these days. If anything, we are encouraged to give in to our desires. Glossy ads urge us to 'indulge' or 'treat' ourselves, to splash out on luxury items, to chase our dreams – in short, to do whatever we want, as long as we're not deliberately harming anyone. So this account of the temptation of Jesus might not immediately resonate with a modern audience. Why should it matter if Jesus uses his power and privilege to gain prestige for himself? Why wouldn't he want to look upon 'all the kingdoms of the world' from a lofty height? But Jesus calls out the temptations for what they are – empty, distorted promises that go against everything he is. Jesus does not look down on people but accompanies them. He does not live for himself but in service of others.

During Lent, we are invited to take stock of our direction in life, to reflect on what temptations or stumbling blocks might be holding us back. The 'me-first' messaging of our culture encourages a reductive understanding of what it means to be a responsible human. It is not enough to float through life as though our indulgences are the most important thing and our actions do not have consequences. Jesus calls us to engage with the world, to put others first, to use our privilege for the benefit of others rather than ourselves. Auschwitz survivor Elie Wiesel has spoken of the dangers of becoming indifferent to the world: 'Indifference can be tempting – more than that, seductive. It is so much easier to look away from victims. It is so much easier to avoid such rude interruptions to our work, our dreams, our hopes.'[44] The temptation to indifference and complacency is ever-present. We are reminded this Lent that we are called to a new way of living that is focused outside of ourselves and rooted in love and service.

> **❝**Indifference is more dangerous than anger and hatred ... Indifference is not a response. Indifference is not a beginning; it is an end. And, therefore, indifference is always the friend of the enemy, for it benefits the aggressor – never his victim, whose pain is magnified when he or she feels forgotten.
>
> – Elie Wiesel[45]

Go Deeper

🐦 Lent is a time for honest reflection, to ask ourselves uncomfortable questions. When have I turned away from the suffering of another?

🐦 Sometimes indifference can come from feeling paralysed or overwhelmed by the enormity of a crisis. Small actions can help us move out of this spiral. Think about what steps you might take this Lent to engage with an issue in your community. How can you be of service?

Second Sunday of Lent

Matthew 17:1–9

'It is good for us to be here'

Today's gospel describes an overwhelming experience for three of the disciples, Peter, James and John – Jesus' 'inner circle'. Jesus has been talking about his impending death and resurrection and about the challenges of discipleship (Mt 16:13–27). It's an intense chapter in their friendship with Jesus, and now they have an opportunity for time alone with him. Mountains are important locations in Matthew's Gospel, associated with divine revelation, places where heaven touches earth. The trio realise there is something deeper going on as Jesus is transformed before their eyes. The presence of Moses (representing the Law) and Elijah (representing the prophets) invites parallels between these figures and Jesus, who fulfils both the Law and the prophets.

'It is good for us to be here.' These words of Peter recognise the enormity of the moment. Life is full of opportunities to acknowledge and appreciate the presence of God and others. 'It's great to see you.' 'Thanks for coming.' We pause with gratitude when we welcome a loved one, particularly if we haven't seen them in a while. Think of the joyful reunions after the COVID-19 pandemic had abated, and we could visit and hug our loved ones again. How often do we take a moment with God to simply say, 'Here I am'? Lent gives us that opportunity to press pause and come into the presence of God.

Every moment holds the gift of God's presence. Sometimes this is referred to as the 'sacrament of the present moment'[46], a realisation that God is not 'out there' but here and now, in this time and place. We encounter God in both the extraordinary and ordinary moments of life. In times of laughter and joy, when we delight in our loved ones, God is to be found. In times of rest and reflection, God is within. So while we might not identify with the disciples' experience of the Transfiguration Jesus, if we are attentive to the present moment, we may just find that our world is ablaze with divine love.

"Too often we are not present to the beauty, love, and grace that brim within the ordinary moments of our lives ... The secret to prayer is not to try to make God present, but to make ourselves present to God.

– Ron Rolheiser[47]

Go Deeper

- Bring to mind a happy reunion or a time when you really appreciated the presence of a loved one. Give thanks for the gift of that person.

- This Lent, resolve to become more aware of God's presence in the ordinary moments. Remember that you don't have to go anywhere to find God. Find some space in your day and begin your prayer with the words, 'It is good for us to be here.'

Third Sunday of Lent

John 4:5–42

Partners in mission

The lengthy dialogue between Jesus and the Samaritan woman is one of the most intriguing encounters of the Gospels. The woman is aware of the cultural barriers being crossed. 'How is it that you, a Jew, ask a drink of me, a woman of Samaria?' she asks. Jesus makes a request of her before he offers her anything, implying a level of equality; the woman is an active rather than passive participant in his ministry. They develop a rapport, discussing 'living water', the differences between their religious customs, and the promise of the Messiah. As they talk, the woman moves from calling Jesus 'a Jew' to addressing him as 'Sir', then to recognising him as a 'prophet', and finally to announcing him to others as 'Messiah'. As their connection deepens, she grows in understanding, and her testimony is authentic and convincing. Soon, others are drawn to him.

The encounter breaks religious and social taboos, but Jesus casually engages the woman in conversation as if it's the most natural thing in the world. He recognises her as an individual with a life story and a context of her own. There is intimacy in this encounter. She is deeply affected by his openness and his teaching, and becomes a crucial witness. Jesus uses the metaphor of the harvest to indicate his mission that includes the Samaritans. The time for the harvest has come, he tells the disciples, and this woman represents that movement outwards. What is beautiful about today's gospel is the way Jesus goes about winning hearts: meeting this woman where she is, transcending boundaries, listening and allowing space for questions and debate. It's a more gentle model for Lent than we might be used to.

" This woman is a partner first in conversation, then in mission. The story liberates women for discipleship. It should be read as one of the great missionary texts of the church … The woman does not wait for permission. She is the bearer of good news and she will proclaim it.

– Anne Thurston[48]

Go Deeper

- Set aside some time this week to re-read this passage. Try to place yourself in the shoes of the woman as she talks with Jesus. Trace the stages she goes through, from surprise to belief to excitement. Can you identify with these stages in your own faith journey?

- Jesus treats this woman as an equal, sending her out as a partner in mission. Several times in the Gospels, he transcends expectations about traditional women's roles. What is this saying to a patriarchal Church today, 2000 years later?

Fourth Sunday of Lent

John 9:1–41

'He has opened my eyes'

Today's gospel is long but so worth it. John's narrative is enticing and reads like a piece of theatre, so much so in fact, some scholars think it may actually have been acted out, as it has such clear roles and great one-liners. In the first part we see that the disciples are not really interested in helping the man born blind, they are more concerned with solving the riddle of whose fault it is that he is blind in the first place. Is it divine retribution? Jesus is clear that no one is to blame. God is not vengeful. Jesus focuses on what good God can do through difficult situations. They present an opportunity for God's love and grace to work, not an opportunity for condemnation.

One really interesting thing to notice in the story is how the man's vision increases as the story unfolds. It's not only his physical sight that returns, but spiritually he begins to *see* more and more clearly, despite being faced with fierce opposition from the authorities. In contrast to this clarity, the opposite is happening for the religious leaders. They appear to become even more blind as the story hurtles towards its climax. Those in authority object to the man's newfound vision. While Jesus disappears for most of this narrative, the blind man takes centre stage and grows from seeing Jesus as a prophet, to a man of God and finally to worshipping him.[49]

There are times in our own lives when we need greater clarity. Perhaps we are having difficulties with friends or family members and long to share with them on a deeper level but find it too difficult. We plead with the Lord for greater awareness on how to approach them, knowing that we, too, may face opposition and difficult questioning. At those moments Jesus can certainly seem absent. It is often at these moments of aloneness that Jesus appears. There are many things that we are blind to. We all suffer from some sort of

70

spiritual blindness. Today, let us pray for greater clarity and awareness so that we, like the blind man, may come to see more clearly.

> **As you start to walk on the way, the way appears.**
>
> — Rumi[50]

Go Deeper

- Recall a moment where you gained a greater clarity, greater 'seeing' or awareness. What insights did you receive? What grace was revealed to you?
- Jesus is the role model responding to the blind man with compassion, healing and love. He is the light which guides to greater awareness. What situations in your own life are in need of a similar response? Speak to the Lord about them now.

Fifth Sunday of Lent

John 11:1–45

'I am going there to awaken him'

In today's dramatic narrative we read how Jesus is surrounded by a culture of death. The disciples are afraid to go back to Bethany because Jesus' opponents want to stone him to death,[51] Mary and Martha are distraught over the death of their brother, and Lazarus himself lies bound in the darkness of the tomb. It appears as if there is no hope as even Jesus weeps, sharing in this grief and distress as he stands before the tomb of Lazarus. If Lazarus represents anything, he represents all of humanity, and the tomb holds all of the situations of death in our world: grief, poverty, heartache, war, injustice, despair, brokenness.

In our own lives feelings of anxiety, resentment and worry can imprison us. The good news is we do not have to live in despair. The story of Lazarus invites all of us to resurrection in the here and now! Jesus calls us out of the tomb and into the fullness of life, to experience the consolation of God's love and peace today, not somewhere far off in the future. It is often easier to remain in the tomb, we tell ourselves, 'This will do', but Jesus wants more for us and says, 'Lazarus, come forth.' To the people Jesus demands, 'Unbind him, let him go', and then, 'They took away the stone.' In this story of liberation we are given a new insight into the power of faith and love. During Lent, this is a message for us all to turn away from a culture of death, to help unbind one another and to allow ourselves and others to emerge into the light. To be saved in this sense is to be made well, to experience restoration. In the global sense it means acknowledging that 'Injustice is not invincible' (*Laudato Si'*, 74). At the heart of this story is the fact that love can conquer all, even death and despair. We can all share in this risen life, in love and peace, today. Jesus comes so that we may live life to the full (Jn 10:10).

"**In confronting the tomb of Lazarus, Jesus confronts every culture of death throughout history, including our own. Here marks the end of greed, poverty, executions, nuclear weapons, environmental destruction and every injustice. And it falls to us, following the example of the non violent Jesus, to carry on the work until it is fulfilled.**

– John Dear[52]

Go Deeper

- Mary and Martha plead with Jesus, then they grieve, and then they almost resist the possibility of new life. It's too much for them. Can you relate to experiences of this in your own life?

- What comes to mind when you think of a culture of death? Where do you see people trying to move the stone? Where do you see people liberated, free to live in the fullness of life?

Palm Sunday

Matthew 26:14–27:66

'Stay awake with me'

Today we meet Jesus in the Garden of Gethsemane, 'grieved and agitated' as he wrestles with the prospect of death. The cross is visibly present in our world, where oppressive systems crucify people, where war and terror inflict death and suffering, where environmental destruction endangers the very fabric of our planet. Here too we meet the crucified Jesus, plummeting into the depths of situations where even God seems absent. But we also look for those who 'hunger and thirst for righteousness', those who stand against oppressive systems even though the path is dangerous and lonely. In today's narrative we meet Simon of Cyrene, who helps Jesus to carry the cross, Joseph of Arimathea, who comes to the aid of Jesus' friends in their darkest hours, the two women who stay with Jesus until the end, Mary, his mother, and Mary Magdalene, sitting outside the tomb when all others have fled.

When Russia invaded Ukraine in early 2022, the world looked on in horror at the death and destruction inflicted on innocent people, but we also saw the outpouring of love and solidarity offered to the millions of refugees created by this war. The helpers were out in force: parents who left buggies at train stations, aid convoys from all over Europe, millions of euros raised. The American TV host, Fred Rogers, once said, 'When I was a boy and I would see scary things in the news, my mother would say to me, "Look for the helpers. You will always find people who are helping."' The many small acts of kindness shown in the aftermath of terrible events add up to a greater movement. Our only response to terror and prejudice must be increasing love and solidarity. Yes, we sit with the horrors of the cross this week, but we can also look for the helpers, and we can be the helpers too.

> **"** Africans believe in something that is difficult to render in English. We call it Ubuntu/botho... You know when it is there and when it is absent. It speaks about humaneness, gentleness, hospitality, putting yourself out on behalf of others, being vulnerable. It embraces compassion and toughness. It recognises that my humanity is bound up in yours, for we can only be human together.
>
> – Desmond Tutu[53]

Go Deeper

- In Gethsemane, Jesus models for believers what the disciples were unable to do, 'stay awake and pray'. When faced with moments of great agony and trial, how do we respond?

- As this Holy Week unfolds, spend time with Matthew's Passion account. Notice the various characters and the roles they play. A good question to ask is 'Where do I stand?' Choose a character in the story to be with and see where it leads you.

🐚 6 🐚

Easter

Introduction to the Easter Season

Alleluia! This is a word you'll be hearing a lot during this Easter Season, which we are now entering. 'Alleluia' is a Hebrew word meaning praise the Lord. This tells us something about the focus of the season, which is characterised by joy and hope. Jesus has risen, and he invites us into this new life. The Easter event illuminates our lives as individuals and communities, calling us to be light for the world. The Season of Easter runs from the Easter Vigil to the Feast of Pentecost, a long period of fifty days. At this time of year, we are aware of the signs of new life around us. The days are longer and brighter, birds are singing, flowers are blooming. The new life that bursts from the earth reminds us that God is the source of all life and goodness. Easter is a time of new beginnings.

Over the coming weeks, we take a detour away from Matthew's Gospel. We turn instead to the Gospel of John, with readings from his account of those who encountered Jesus after he rose from the dead, starting with the women at the tomb. We celebrate with these disciples as they are filled with joy at Jesus' presence, and we share in their struggles as they prepare to take their first steps as witnesses to the Good News of the resurrection. These disciples have a shaky start. They sometimes fail to recognise Jesus. They are afraid, they doubt, they hide. We can identify with their

reactions. Sometimes it is difficult to see God at work in our lives. For that reason, the accounts that we hear over the coming weeks are very reassuring. Even when the disciples don't realise it, Jesus is with them every step of the way. They are made new by his presence, and their fear is replaced by faith. When we meet the risen Christ, we are new creations.

The Easter message is for everyone, whatever our situation. It is never too late to make a fresh start. The good news is that Jesus is with us. He is present when we pray and when we struggle to pray, when we are happy and when we are hurting, in the beauty of our world, which is always being made new, and in the goodness and love we share with others. As we make our way through this new season, we open the door and invite the risen Jesus to enter.

Easter Vigil

Matthew 28:1–10

In between

At the beginning of tonight's gospel is an empty space. When Mary Magdalene and 'the other Mary' (mother of James and Joseph) go to the tomb, early morning after the Sabbath, they are greeted with the words, 'He is not here; for he has been raised, as he said.' They are invited to look inside the tomb. For now, this empty space is their only link between the cross and resurrection, between death and life. The angel tells the women not to be afraid. But they leave the tomb 'quickly with fear and great joy', the depths and heights of emotion carrying them onwards to tell the other disciples. It's only when they meet the risen Jesus that they truly believe.

Matthew's is the only Gospel that mentions the sabbath, that full day between the evening on Calvary and the morning at the tomb. He includes the detail that the religious leaders approach Pilate to secure the tomb, but we hear nothing of the disciples. As we enter Holy Saturday, we are in this in-between space, 'a pregnant emptiness, a silent nothing which says everything'.[54] And then, at our vigil, this empty space is filled with light! Out of the cross and the empty tomb come joy, hope and abundant life.

Our human experience sometimes brings us to a place where the veil between life and death is thin and exposed. When we have a brush with death through accident or illness, when a loved one is rushed to hospital or undergoing surgery and we are waiting for news, we are suspended in that 'in-between' place between life and death, light and darkness. As we share the light of Christ with one another this evening, we remember that as Christ is light for the world, we are light for one another. We sit with one another when life is difficult and uncertain, and we walk with one another in hope, offering a glimpse of the light that is beyond the shadows.

‘The gloom of the world is but a shadow; behind it, yet within reach, is joy. Take joy. There is a radiance and glory in the darkness could we but see, and to see we have only to look. I beseech you to look!’

– Fra Giovanni[55]

Go Deeper

- Think of a time when you experienced uncertainty, an 'in-between' time when you were unsure how things would work out. What brought you hope – perhaps a loved one was present to bring light to the darkness?

- Sharing the Christ-light with one another is a reminder that we are called to be light for the world, as an individuals and in communities. What can we do in our own lives to bring light to dark situations?

Easter Sunday

John 20:1–9

Dare to hope

The empty tomb causes consternation. In John's account, Mary Magdalene, the first to arrive, is confused by the missing stone, 'They have taken the Lord.' Peter and John see the empty tomb and wrappings, but appear not to understand. Only when John enters the tomb does he 'see and believe'. Mary Magdalene will be the first to see the risen Jesus, recognising him when he calls her by name. Later, Thomas will be convinced only when he sees and touches Jesus. The Good News dawns gradually for the disciples. We share in their awe and excitement this morning. Jesus is alive! We enter into the mystery, allowing ourselves to believe and to hope.

You may have heard the expression 'the audacity of hope'. It became famous as the title of Barack Obama's autobiography, but it originated in a sermon by pastor Jeremiah Wright in which he reflected on the G. F. Watts painting, 'Hope'. In the painting, a female figure sits, blindfolded, playing a lyre that has only one string. 'With her clothes in rags, her body scarred and bruised and bleeding, her harp all but destroyed and with only one string left, she had the audacity to make music and praise God ... To take the one string you have left and to have the audacity to hope ... that's the real word God will have us hear.'[56] The mystery of the resurrection is that we can dare to hope. God has made all things new.

The resurrection completes what Jesus began. The resurrection of Jesus, who was persecuted, suffered and died, is God's affirmation that victory does not rest with the world's victors, but with its victims. Jesus' words and deeds are risen and exalted too. The Jesus who is raised is the one who sides with the poor, the mistreated, the ignored; who challenges the status quo and tells us 'the last will be first'. We are challenged to model our lives on this vision of Jesus, to shine light into the darkness and bring hope to an uncertain world.

"Jesus' death was an interruption in his ministry, not the point of it.

– Daneen Akers[57]

Go Deeper

- Think of a time when you were moved by a person or event, while perhaps not fully understanding why. Reflecting back, what insights are there? What did you learn?

- With the world in chaos, it can be difficult to hope. The resurrection shows us that even the most desperate situations can be redeemed. Where do you see hope in the world?

Second Sunday of Easter

John 20:19–31

Shalom

We do not come through suffering and difficult times unscarred. We are changed by them. Often they bring some sort of growth into our lives, and usually it is not a pleasant experience. The risen Jesus bears the wounds of his suffering and in today's gospel invites Thomas to get in touch with this reality. Would it not have made more sense for John to write the wounds out of this story? No, because here we tap into the great mystery of this narrative: we can experience resurrection and still bear the signs of 'wounded-ness'. The cross and new life are deeply intertwined. We can be healed, fully transformed, yet the scars of what has happened remain, almost like a reminder of how far we have come. When we recall times of our own 'wounded-ness' do we also hear Jesus' 'peace be with you'? This peace, this *Shalom*, is more than a wish for a peaceful day. It expresses the desire that the person receiving the blessing might be whole in body, mind and spirit. The risen Jesus brings a peace that is life-giving.

In difficult times, becoming aware of Christ's presence amongst us can open our hearts. We keep going in confidence that any suffering we are experiencing is not the end of the story. For the disciples this experience moves them from being closed off to the world to rejoicing, and this in turn opens up the mission for them to be unending witnesses to God's love, to be for others what Jesus has been for them. The risen Jesus is active in all our lives and in the world around us. May we be open to transformation, to growth and to sharing this life-giving Spirit with others.

" For even if the whole world believed in resurrection, little would change until we began to practice it. We can believe in CPR, but people will remain dead until someone breathes new life into them.

– Shane Claiborne[58]

Go Deeper

- When have you experienced resurrection or healing in your own life yet still carried the signs of your woundedness?

- 'These are written so that you may come to believe ...' Through the Word we come to know Jesus more deeply. How has the Word of God nourished you in your own life? How do you experience the Word of God in your life?

Third Sunday of Easter

Luke 24:13–35

'Their eyes were opened'

The disciples on the road today are a jumbled mess of emotions, 'astounded', 'sad', and it is no wonder. Their friend and teacher has been brutally killed, along with their hopes and expectations, and now there are strange reports of a missing body. They have left the chaotic crowds, the violence and devastation behind them. An experience like this, of complete desolation, affects one's entire being. We become closed in on ourselves, consumed by anger or grief, and it can be very difficult to see Christ walking beside us. It can even cloud our memories of times when we did experience God's love and grace in the past. We can feel like we are spiralling downwards, cut off.

We read in the narrative today that something shifts for the disciples in the midst of their deep anguish and pain. A 'stranger' falls into step with them, and this is no ordinary encounter. Jesus walks with them, even though at first they do not recognise him. He listens to their pain, and he does not interrupt them. When they are finished he puts their story into the context of a wider vision; he breaks through to them. When we experience desolation we often need another person to help open our eyes and remind us of who we truly are. This person might be an *anam cara* (soul friend), someone who truly *hears* us and puts our story compassionately into the context of the bigger picture of our lives. This can be consoling. It is through experiences of great suffering (unfortunately) and also great love, that God's light shines through. The disciples recognise Jesus in the breaking of the bread; their 'eyes were opened', their 'hearts burned'. The words of the scriptures and the enlightening meal go hand in hand, illuminating a new reality. New energy is found, and they go bouncing back to Jerusalem; the place of death and pain is now transformed, and they are bursting to tell their companions.

> **"**The old news about Easter is that it is about resurrection. The new news may be that it is not so much about the resurrection of Jesus as it is about our own ... Jesus, you see, is already gone from one tomb. The only question now is whether or not we are willing to abandon our own.
>
> – Joan Chittister[59]

Go Deeper

- Enter into the Emmaus story with the disciples and Jesus as they walk. Whatever your truth is today, share this with Jesus: your dreams, your heartache, your reality. Allow him to speak to you.
- Can you remember a time when your 'eyes were opened'? What Word was spoken to you? By whom? What food did you receive?

Fourth Sunday of Easter

John 10:1–10

Abundant life

Some years ago, Pope Francis grabbed people's attention with a vivid image when he urged priests to become shepherds who smell of their sheep: 'This I ask you,' he said, 'be shepherds, with the "odour of the sheep", make it real, as shepherds among your flock.'[60] He was echoing the language of the Gospels where Jesus speaks of himself as the 'good shepherd' who knows his sheep, calls his sheep by name. There is a beautiful line in today's gospel, 'the sheep follow him because they know his voice'. This kind of trust could only be gained by a shepherd who stays close to their sheep, feeds and protects them. In today's passage we are invited into a deep relationship with Jesus, the good shepherd, to spend time with him, to listen for his voice, a voice that brings peace and comfort. From this relationship comes life, abundant life. In contrast to a thief whose only motive is to take, Jesus gives life that is joyful, hopeful, meaningful and eternal.

As Christ is shepherd to us, we are called to be shepherds to others. We do not help anyone by engaging in 'saviourism', whereby we swoop in and try to 'make a difference' without getting to know the people we wish to support or what is really needed. It is far more meaningful to develop close bonds over time, like the good shepherd. Pope Francis invites us to 'go out of ourselves', to go beyond our own boundaries and be present to people, to really get to know each other and build friendships, to lift each other up. The 'abundant' life is an ongoing process of walking together, working together, learning to trust one another – maybe stumbling or making mistakes, but always working to live in harmony. As followers of the Good Shepherd, we live so that all may 'have life, and have it abundantly'.

"When we say that we want to go to the margins, what we are implying (consciously or not) is that those we're going to are 'other' than us ... so it's not so much that the Church reaches out to the margins but that the Church needs to reach out beyond OUR margins. We need to go beyond our own, self-imposed, boundaries.

– Jim Deeds[61]

Go Deeper

- Jesus, the Good Shepherd, wants to speak to our hearts. How do you seek to hear Jesus' voice? What obstacles in your life might prevent you from hearing it?

- What does the expression 'abundant life' conjure up for you? When do you feel most alive, joyful, energised, in tune with the universe and with God? Reflect this week also on how you might live this 'abundant life' in community.

Fifth Sunday of Easter

John 14:1–12

'I am the Way'

Philip and Thomas are desperate to understand more fully where Jesus is going. They want to know how they can get there, what God is like, and how can they see God. Big questions that show their deep desire to know God more intimately. Jesus urges the disciples to embrace the journey, the Way that lies ahead of them, rather than focusing on the destination. For it is only in the light of the events that will happen to them (and us) that any period of time can be fully understood. In the past the phrase 'I am the Way, the Truth and the Life ...' may have been used to exclude those who did not consider themselves followers of Christ, but this is a distortion of a beautiful text. Jesus is the Way because he *models* the Way for us, and we are invited to follow.

We read throughout the Scriptures that people experienced God in different ways. For Moses it was in a burning bush or a cloud; for Elijah it was a whisper; for Solomon and Joseph it was in a dream.

Philip wants to see God, and the response he receives is that God can be experienced in the here and now, for to know Jesus is to know God (Jn 1:1–18). Jesus, through his life, shows us what the presence of God in this world looks like and, at the same time, what it means to be fully human. Through him we see that God is loving, inclusive, embracing of all people, compassionate. Jesus invites us to contemplate this mystery of God's presence in him, 'I am in the Father and the Father is in me...' We are invited to become more aware of this truth today, that the sacred is present in the material universe, in human form, in created matter, and through Jesus we can come to see this more deeply.

" The Eternal Christ is thus revealed
as the map, the blueprint, the
promise, the pledge, the guarantee
of what is happening everywhere, all
summed up in one person so we can
see it in personified form

– Richard Rohr[62]

Go Deeper

🐚 Jesus wants us to experience deep peace, in the
here and now. Talk to him about your concerns.
Hear Jesus speaking these words to you, 'Do not
let your hearts be troubled.'

🐚 Contemplative practices such as *Lectio Divina* (see
page 14) can help us to experience the living Christ
in our daily lives and help us to follow the Way, the
Truth and the Life he sets out before us. Allow
the words of this Gospel to soak deeply into your
heart. Pick a phrase which stands out for you and
use it as a mantra this week.

Sixth Sunday of Easter

John 14:15–21

'And you in me and I in you'

We continue to read this Sunday from the Farewell Discourse of John's Gospel (chapters 14–17) where Jesus is consoling the disciples, 'I will not leave you orphaned.' Jesus tells the disciples that he will send an 'advocate' (*parak-lētos*) to them. This term is only found in John's writings[63] and translates as a helper, a comforter, someone we call to our aid. Jesus has been this advocate for the disciples, but now he will be present for them in a different way, dwelling amongst them, dwelling in them, *in-dwelling*. This in turn calls for a loving response from the disciples and from all followers of Christ.

In a famous reflection, Joseph Whelan SJ wrote about this type of love; he said, 'Nothing is more practical than finding God, than falling in Love in a quite absolute, final way.' This love will decide everything, what gets you up in the morning, how you spend your time, what breaks your heart, what amazes you. Whelan says, 'Fall in Love, stay in love, and it will decide everything.'[64] Experiencing something of this indwelling presence of God and keeping God's commandments are deeply interconnected. This love *will* decide everything because it must flow outwards, be lived out in our daily lives, for it cannot be contained.

The words of the gospel today are deeply intimate, they cannot be understood with the head, only with the heart. As we spend time with them we begin to realise that it is not just the disciple's story, it is also our story, a story we experience on a deep level. It is another reminder to us that all beings are sacred, all beings carry divine DNA within. Let us begin again to see God present within ourselves, in others and in all of creation.

❝ We are not human beings having a spiritual experience. We are spiritual beings having a human experience.

– Pierre Teilhard de Chardin

Go Deeper

🍂 What prevents you from growing in deeper awareness of God's indwelling presence in yourself and in others? Some possibilities might be everyday concerns, busyness or a lack of space or silence.

🍂 Recall a moment of grace where you saw your life as sacred, aware of Christ's presence within. What happened? What emotions were there? What was your response?

Feast of the Ascension

Matthew 28:16–20

'Go therefore...'

As is common in Matthew's Gospel, we find ourselves with Jesus on a mountain – an important setting for Matthew in moments of divine revelation. The eleven male disciples have been instructed by the female disciples, the two Marys, to go to Galilee to see the risen Jesus. In Matthew's account, the male disciples have not visited the tomb or seen Jesus up to this point. These women, the first witnesses to the resurrection, pass the message on to the men. This 'passing on' is an important theme as it sets the scene for the 'Great Commission', Jesus handing over his mission to the disciples.

When they see Jesus, the group has a typical mixed response: as always, they are an imperfect bunch. Yet Jesus tasks them to 'make disciples of all nations'. We remember that early in Matthew's Gospel, Galilee was referred to as 'Galilee of the Gentiles' (Mt 4:15), so it is fitting that the inclusive mission to all nations begins here. Matthew often thinks in terms of 'delegated powers'[65]: Jesus has authority to teach – as noted by the crowds (Mt 7:29) – and this authority is now passed on to the disciples. When he first sent the disciples out he gave them authority over unclean spirits and illnesses (Mt 10:1). Now, the mission is extended outwards to all nations.

We are the extension of this commissioning. God's kingdom is not limited to a particular place or set of people. Our communities are called to be alive not inside buildings but on the streets, constantly reaching out. Jesus' mission is all-encompassing, infinitely wide, infinitely open. His final message is a promise to us all: 'I am with you always, to the end of the age.' We might recall here the promise in Jesus' name *Emmanuel*, 'God with us' (Mt 1:23). The risen Jesus has not abandoned the world but is in this world, the divine presence in the community, and his followers are sent to carry this love to the world.

" Christ opened the path to us. He is like a roped guide climbing a mountain who, on reaching the summit, pulls us up to him and leads us to God. If we entrust our life to him, if we let ourselves be guided by him, we are certain to be in safe hands.

– Pope Francis[66]

Go Deeper

- 'I am with you always until the end of the age...' Stay with this text this week. How does it make you feel? Where do you notice Christ present in the world around you?

- How do you, as a disciple of the Risen Lord, feel called to bring faith, hope and love to others?

Pentecost Sunday

John 20:19–23

Breath of life

In his final moments on the cross, before he took his last breath, Jesus entrusted his mother and his beloved disciple to each other, establishing a new family for those he loved and held close in life. Now, Jesus breathes his Spirit into this new community, a new creation. In spite of Mary Magdalene's testimony that she has 'seen the Lord', the disciples are afraid and hiding. Jesus comes to dispel their fear, his first word a message and manifestation of peace: *Shalom*. Several times, Jesus had promised his friends that he would send them the Holy Spirit ('Advocate') to remind them of everything he taught (Jn 14:26) and to guide them to truth (Jn 16:13). This Spirit is Jesus present with them, in a new way, bringing them to new life.

We read that Jesus 'breathed on them'. This breath of life is the same lifeforce that sustains us at every moment, connecting us to everyone and everything – the plants that give off oxygen, the air breathed by all living beings in the past, present and future. This is the sacrament of life that God breathed into Adam and Ezekiel[67], breath that gives and sustains life. It is this breath that God breathes into each and every one of us. It is no wonder, then, that many spiritual practices invite us to focus on our breath to become more present, because it is in the present we find God and this life-giving Spirit.

In the creation accounts, we read that a 'wind from God' (Gen 1:2) swept over the primordial chaos. The Hebrew word used for wind is '*ruach*', also translated as Spirit, the creative aspect of God. The Spirit is God's continuing presence in our world today. She is not confined to time or place, but dwells in everyone and is present in every culture and age. She is a gentle comforter and a vibrant guide, 'inspiring the prophets of each century to speak the word of God as it emerges newly and freshly in every age'.[68]

"The hovering Spirit, who has been brooding over the chaotic waters since the beginning of time, is searching out landing space, lifeboats, lighthouses, where this same Spirit can infiltrate, can put the counter-cultural plan in train, so that eventually the divine safety operation for the planet will succeed.

– Mark Patrick Hederman[69]

Go Deeper

Create space for meditation this week, beginning with five minutes each day. Focus on your breath. As you breathe in, inhale the breath of life – a gift from God, a gift from the earth, given by the plants and the trees; as you breathe out, exhale your gift to the world – with your breath you feed the plants and trees, you bless the world around you.

Trinity Sunday

John 3:16–18

Divine energy

'God so loved the world ...' Our short gospel passage today is familiar. It is known as one of the most concise expressions of Christian faith. Jesus is speaking to Nicodemus,[70] a Jewish leader who has come to him with a series of questions. We, too, seek to understand who Jesus is. Jesus explains that the key to the mystery is love: God loved the world so much that God became one of us. The creative love of God, in the world and part of the world since the beginning of time (Jn 1:3, 10), reaches its climax in the incarnation.

Something of this creative love is expressed in the parent–child relationship. The all-encompassing love of a parent for their child is a model of the intimacy between creator and creature. A parent wants the best for a child, to hold them close, to protect them from harm, to fill them with love and hope. The inseparable bond between a mother and the child she has carried and nurtured in her body has an energy of its own. As the child grows, the love between parent and child continues to flow, sustaining the child, connecting them always with the love from whence they came. In a similar way, the Spirit weaves and flows through our lives, joining us with the source of divine love.

The mystery of the Trinity is that God is a relationship of love. And Jesus is the way into this great mystery of God's presence in creation, in our world, in ourselves, in one another. 'Jesus is the model and metaphor for all of creation being drawn into this infinite flow of love.'[71] Through Jesus, God invites us into the divine nature, so we can share and participate in it. We are 'pulsing with divine energy'[72], and on this foundation we build our lives of love.

"There is nothing the baby does that is not delightful to the parents. Whether playing, sleeping, dribbling ... sucking a nipple, a thumb or a toe, there is beautiful meaning for the adoring mother. So with us and God. Even the most ordinary and routine actions and duties of our roles in life, may be the most sacred of all. The mystery of God is experienced as a paradox. The Holy Spirit spins gold from the bare threads of our threadbare days.

– Daniel O'Leary[73]

Go Deeper

Love seeks expression. When you love someone, you identify with that person. You want to be close to them, and you want to give them everything, your very self. Reflect this week on this short verse and how it speaks to you of God's love: 'God so loved the world that he gave his only Son'.

97

Feast of Corpus Christi

John 6:51–58

Broken people

Several cities around the world, including Vatican City, have a 'Homeless Jesus' statue. The sculptures, created by artist Tim Schmalz, depict Jesus as a homeless person, asleep on a park bench. The face of the blanketed figure is obscured, but the wounds on his feet reveal his identity. In Dublin, the statue is located on the grounds of Christ Church Cathedral; however, a poll in a national newspaper found that readers would have preferred Molesworth Street, at a location near where homeless man Jonathan Corrie had died. The forty-three-year-old had been sleeping rough in a doorway, just metres from the Irish government buildings. Speaking about the sculpture, Schmalz said, 'Jesus did not say "love the wealthy". His ministry was to the suffering and the poor. The heart of Christianity is to love the broken people, and this is where you find Jesus.'

In today's gospel, Jesus speaks of himself as the 'living bread'. This extract is part of a much longer passage in which Jesus reveals the intimacy of his relationship with us. Just as bread nourishes us physically, Jesus, the 'bread of life', nourishes us spiritually. In Hebrew, the expression 'flesh and blood' refers to the whole being. The gift of bread is Jesus himself, whose body was broken on the cross. It is this 'broken' Jesus that we meet in the Eucharist, and who meets us in our own broken state. This broken Jesus challenges us to love the broken people we meet. The representation of Jesus as a homeless person challenges us to reflect on the paradox of the broken, marginalised Jesus, who gives us life. May we see and love him in others.

" God uses broken things. It takes broken soil to produce a crop, broken clouds to give rain, broken grain to give bread, broken bread to give strength.

– Vance Havner[74]

Go Deeper

There are homeless people in all our cities and towns. People sleep rough, and there is also 'invisible' homelessness. Find out what plans and initiatives there are in your area to support people in these situations. Can you write to your local representative, or volunteer for a charity that tackles homelessness?

We have all been hurt or broken in some way; our brokenness binds us together as humans. Jesus challenges us to love the broken people. We start with ourselves.

❧ 7 ❧
Ordinary Time (2)

Eighth Sunday in Ordinary Time

Matthew 6:24–34

Mind the gap

Each of us experiences worries and anxieties from time to time, ranging from the small stuff to conjuring up worst-case scenarios. This can take a real toll on people's physical, emotional and mental health. As Jesus says in the gospel today, is worrying going to add an hour to your life? No, but it can certainly contribute to taking hours away from your lifespan. God's Word consoles us today as Jesus invites us to turn and look at nature. By bringing our attention to the 'birds of the air' and the 'lilies of the field', we are reawakened to the simplicity and abundance of life. In a very practical sense, this gospel invites us to a freedom of spirit where we do not focus on accumulating wealth or possessions. This call to live simply is not inviting us to be naive or careless. Nor does it show disregard for the struggles of those on the poverty line. On the contrary, Matthew's Gospel is deeply concerned with justice for the poor. Rather, this text invites us to reorient our values, to look at our real needs and free ourselves of attachment to what is unnecessary.

Followers of Jesus are called to a radical letting go of attachment to material things. This letting go is counter-cultural in today's world. We have been sold a very different narrative by the corporate world, bombarded by messages that tell us what products are 'essential' for our happiness. The Gospel takes a different view. What really makes us happy cannot be bought. Consumerism in our world thrives because we are not at peace with ourselves, and we sometimes try to fill that gap with 'stuff'. This fuels anxiety and worries about many things because it prevents us from living in the present, instead we are oriented towards accumulating for an unknown future. This is a false narrative, one that has literally cost us the Earth. Today's gospel gives us permission to say 'enough' and to embrace a more simple lifestyle. We are so much more than consumers! We are beloved children of a generous, loving God, and it is in this we are invited to place our trust today.

> **"Worrying is carrying tomorrow's load with today's strength – carrying two days at once ... Worrying doesn't empty tomorrow of its sorrow, it empties today of its strength.**
>
> – Corrie ten Boom[75]

Go Deeper

- How do you react to worries or problems? What happens in your body, mind and heart? Trusting your worries to God is more than a cliche, it can be liberating. Journaling is one way to do this. Try it this week.

- Observing nature can reveal God to us in beautiful ways. Consider the practice of *Lectio Divina with Nature* this week. See page 133.

Ninth Sunday in Ordinary Time

Matthew 7:21–27

Wholehearted

The Sermon on the Mount, which began with a series of blessings, ends with a series of warnings from Jesus. The subject is something we don't like to think about too much – judgement – who will 'enter the kingdom of heaven', and what does this mean? The short parable of the builders might shed some light. Jesus' listeners would have been well aware that the durability of a house depended primarily on the land on which it was built. In typical parable style, we are faced with two opposing ways – the rock and the sand, representing the wise people who take Jesus' words to heart and the foolish who ignore his words. Both groups 'hear' the same message, but just as words (calling out 'Lord Lord') are not enough, neither is simply hearing. What matters is action, specifically, acting on 'these words of mine'.

It's probably fair to assume that Jesus is referring here to all that he has said during the lengthy Sermon on the Mount (Mt 5:1–7:29). The central teaching of this sermon, the Beatitudes, offers an invitation into the life of God, in the here and now. So while Jesus appears to be talking here about what we might call the 'final judgement', we are reminded that the kingdom of heaven is not a far-off goal to aim for or a way of speaking about the after-life. It is an inner transformation, a way of being in the world modelled on God's limitless love and mercy.

If we limit our faith practice to religious obligation or academic learning ('hearing'), prayer ('Lord Lord') or public acts ('deeds of power'), we have missed the crucial element, we have built our house on sand. That is not kingdom faith. We cannot separate the truth of what we believe from how we live. We are called to conversion, a wholehearted response to Jesus, an embodiment of the beatitude values, and a life modelled on God's immeasurable love.

"Ministry is participating in God's dream of a good creation, and Jesus is the model. Do you want to follow Jesus? Or are you content just to worship him, and postpone for just a little longer the fulfilment of the dream of God? ... Kingdom-of-God thinking calls us to risk.

– Verna J. Dozier[76]

Go Deeper

- With this short parable of the builders and the houses built on rock and sand, we are invited to reflect on where we stand. As usual, we might find that it's somewhere in the middle!

- Jesus calls us to an ever-deeper response to his teachings and his love. How does God speak to you, and how do you listen? How does your relationship with God influence your decisions and your actions?

Tenth Sunday in Ordinary Time

Matthew 9:9–13

Mercy me

Today we meet Matthew sitting at a tax booth. Tax collectors were considered despised by society because they were collaborating with the occupying Roman Empire. It was also assumed that they took more than was needed from their own people and pocketed the surplus. Yet, this is who Jesus 'sees' and calls to conversion, and this is a person who recognises Jesus and follows him without question. The narrative then moves to the question of table fellowship. Jesus is surrounded by those that people love to hate and the religious authorities wonder how he can eat with tax collectors and sinners. To be fair to the Pharisees, they are asking these questions because they desire to live holy lives and be true to God's law. So their real question to Jesus today is 'what' or 'who' is holy? Surely not those who collaborate with the enemy?

We are all capable of things that might render us outcast by society, and at times we too find ourselves lost and cut off from the world. It is then we need to be shown God's mercy and love, through the helping hands of our loved ones or our community. In our own weakness and fragility we long for someone to reach out to us, to 'see' us. Jesus reminds the Pharisees that all are worthy, all are holy, all are in need of mercy, including them. Their problem is that they are blind to their own fragility and so unable to offer a helping hand to others. Jesus quotes from the prophet Hosea (6:6) saying, 'I desire mercy not sacrifice'. Mercy is the true sacrifice. Jesus is challenging his hearers to reach out to those who might need a helping hand to 'get up' and move away from that which separates them from others. Something new is going on here, something which is calling us back to the truth of who we are. Jesus does not condemn us. He *sees* us, sometimes sitting in the wrong place, and gently says, come on, this way, follow me.

"Mercy discounts the economic sense of love and faith and care for a person and lives out of a divine sense of love instead. Mercy gives a human being who does not 'deserve' love, love. And why? Because, the Scriptures answer, God knows of what we are made.

– Joan Chittister[77]

Go Deeper

- Who are the people in your community who sit with those considered 'unworthy'?
- Matthew's call comes in the midst of his ordinary everyday life, and he is ready for it. When has someone reached out to you at just the right time? Can you be more conscious or alert to the ways God's grace is working in your life?

11th Sunday in Ordinary Time

Matthew 9:36–10:8

Signs of life

Pope Francis's annual pre-Christmas address to Vatican cardinals has become something of a hit. He is not shy of naming truths that might be hard to hear.[78] During the 2015 address, Pope Francis criticised those who were trying to block reform in the Church and said that changes at the Vatican should be seen first and foremost as a sign of life. The Church needs reform 'because she is alive'.[79] Pope Francis does this from a place of love, as a pastor who has genuine care for people, for the Gospel message and for our common home.

In the gospel today we hear that Jesus has deep compassion for the people, because they are like 'sheep without a shepherd'; with no real spiritual leadership or mentors to guide them they cannot grow in their faith or reach their full potential. The religious and political leaders who are meant to care for their well-being have instead oppressed and exploited them. So when Jesus sends out the Twelve disciples he sends them first to 'the lost sheep of the house of Israel', to the people, yes, but also to the religious leaders of his day. Jesus was a radical reformer, who was concerned at this point not with setting up a new religion but with transforming his own faith community.

Where reform is concerned, there will always be obstacles. These obstacles usually come from within, because reform involves letting go of what no longer serves. The ego finds this difficult. Individually and institutionally, we are in need of conversion and transformation. Conversion enables us to be authentic to the inclusive, communal, and universal message of Jesus. It allows us to deepen and nourish a more authentic spirituality. Today many people are (re)discovering the wisdom traditions in Christianity, turning towards the mystics, returning to practices like *Lectio Divina,* embracing contemplation and silence, reconnecting with treasures we have forgotten (Mt 13) or perhaps were never taught. It is one of the signs that we live in a time of great change and that holding on to that which no longer serves will not help. The Twelve are sent out to heal and revive 'the house' and to let in some fresh air.

> **" Tradition is not a museum, true religion is not a freezer, and doctrine is not static but grows and develops, like a tree that remains the same yet which gets bigger and bears ever more fruit.**
>
> – Pope Francis[80]

Go Deeper

- How do you deal with change? Can we, as individuals and as members of the Church community, learn to see change as a sign of life?
- Do you experience the Church as a place of encounter and dialogue? What can your parish or community do to provide safe spaces for people to discuss, to ask questions and to grow in faith?

12th Sunday in Ordinary Time

Matthew 10:26–33

Noli timere

The last words of the poet Seamus Heaney, in a text to his wife Marie, were the Latin words '*Noli timere*', meaning, don't be afraid. Heaney was doing what poets and writers do best – expressing human fears and anxieties in a way that makes sense of them. His son Mick wrote, 'We seized on his final words as a kind of lifebuoy. It seemed to us that he had encapsulated the swirl of emotion, uncertainty and fear he was facing at the end, and articulated it in a restrained yet inspiring way.'[81] Fear can take many different forms. We worry about our families, our health, financial security. In places troubled by war or famine, there are deeper fears: can I manage to feed my children? Will we have to leave our home in order to be safe? Will we survive? When we're afraid, it's natural to question God, even to lose faith. We might turn to God in prayer, seeking comfort, or we may struggle to pray because we cannot stand the uncertainties of life. Life doesn't always make sense in the moment. Looking back, we gain a deeper perspective. Perhaps that's why Seamus Heaney, close to death, was able to reassure his loved ones.

Jesus acknowledges the worst fears of the disciples when he says, 'Do not fear those who kill the body but cannot kill the soul.' The ultimate fear – fear of death – is addressed head on. Jesus doesn't promise that we will come to no harm, but affirms that God is with us, whatever happens. The comparison with sparrows is almost amusing. Sparrows were of little value, other than as a cheap source of food. Yet God cares so much for the tiny sparrow that not one perishes without God knowing – and we are of more value than 'many sparrows'! God is present in the fear and messiness of life, caring for us so intimately that the hairs on our head are counted.

> "When we travel through those wilderness places of our lives where we feel lost, insecure, lonely, frustrated, discouraged, or overcome by busyness: Help us to trust in You, God of the journey. When we catch glimpses of the tremendous love you have for us and experience a deep, loving connection with others: Help us to trust in You, God of the journey.
>
> – Joyce Rupp[82]

Go Deeper

- Admitting your deepest fears can be daunting. Looking back, what has brought you comfort at a time when you were afraid?

- The sparrow, one of the smallest of birds, is cared for and loved by God. This is a reminder that no matter how insignificant we feel or how challenging the circumstances, God is with us. Today, recall the times or places where you felt God's supporting presence.

13th Sunday in Ordinary Time

Matthew 10:37–42

A cup of water

Offering a cup of water or simple hospitality to a stranger might not seem like much, but that's where Jesus starts. Instructing the Twelve, he tells them that anyone who welcomes them or offers 'even a cup of cold water to one of these little ones' will be rewarded. When we use the term 'little ones', it usually refers to children. In Matthew, it likely describes the community of believers, though it's not clear whether it refers to all disciples, those of low social status, or those weak in faith.[83] Jesus is preparing the disciples and tells them in bleak terms about the cost of discipleship: a life of self-denial, of 'taking up the cross'. But the final part of his instruction is about the virtues of hospitality and compassion. Small acts of kindness have a significance beyond what we expect: 'Whoever welcomes you welcomes me', says Jesus. The disciples will participate fully in his mission, and those who welcome them are also playing their part in building up God's vision for the world.

The desire to do better is an integral part of our Christian journey. We want to live up to what Jesus asks, but sometimes we imagine this will require grand gestures only. But *here* is somewhere we can start. St Thérèse of Lisieux invites us to practise the 'Little Way of Love', to take every opportunity to offer a kind word, a smile or 'any small gesture which sows peace and friendship'. In *Laudato Si'*, Pope Francis reminds us that it is the 'simple daily gestures which break with the logic of violence exploitation and selfishness.'[84] When hundreds of thousands of refugees poured out of Ukraine amid the Russian invasion of 2022, people lined up at borders to offer clothes, food, transport, accommodation. All these kindnesses sow the seeds of a better world. When we reach out in a spirit of welcome and solidarity, the light of Christ is shining.

" Love, overflowing with small gestures of mutual care, is also civic and political, and it makes itself felt in every action that seeks to build a better world. Love for society and commitment to the common good are outstanding expressions of a charity which affects not only relationships between individuals but also 'macro-relationships, social, economic and political ones'.

– Pope Francis[85]

Go Deeper

Can you recall a time when a small gesture meant the world to you? Resolve to carry out at least one random act of kindness this week: give an unexpected compliment, pay for a drink for the person behind you in line, give someone your seat on public transport, help someone who looks lost, send a care package to a nursing home ...

14th Sunday in Ordinary Time

Matthew 11:25–30

'Come to me'

Matthew's Gospel is written in the context of a patriarchal society where men counted and women and children did not. The social reality was that children had no voice. They were invisible. Yet, children are given high visibility in Matthew, and in today's text Jesus puts 'infants' centre stage as the ones who are great examples of humility and wisdom (18:3–5; 19:13–15; 21:15).[86] Jesus praises God for the grace of openness and humility he sees around him, for revealing 'these things' to 'infants'. There is a satisfying reversal of expectations here.

You can search online for nuggets of wisdom from children and the results will warm your heart:

- 'I like wind because it makes everything dance.'
- 'As we walked on the beach for the first time my four year old yelled, "I love being in this world."'
- 'I asked my five year old how his day was and he said, "It was awesome". I asked him why, and he replied, "Because I wanted it to be!"'[87]

The challenge for each of us today is to rekindle a childlike sense of awe and wonder for our world, not to let our hearts become hardened like those of the 'wise' in the Gospel.

For Jesus, God's grace is found in the humble, in those who are open to new possibilities, in those whose hearts are open. We are invited to grow in greater awareness by seeing through the eyes of a child, rather than through the eyes of those who claim to have all the answers.

Jesus desires freedom for each of us so that we can find rest in his love and tenderness and a wisdom for which the soul yearns. In times when we feel exhausted or in despair the final lines of today's gospel are worth spending time with: 'Come to me, all you that are weary ... I am gentle and humble in heart, and you will find rest for your souls.'

> **“Learn the unforced rhythms of grace. I will not lay anything heavy or ill-fitting on you. Keep company with me and you'll learn to live freely and lightly**
>
> – The Message[88]

Go Deeper

Reclaim wonder this week: spend time in nature, be creative through writing, dance to your favourite music, bake something, laugh, be curious each day about something, paint (not the walls), sing, play a game, practise gratitude. Notice what happens in you as you tap into your creative energy and wonder. Write about your experience.

15th Sunday in Ordinary Time

Matthew 13:1–23

Blessed are your ears

Today and in the coming Sundays we will hear the parables from Matthew 13. Parables are more of an experience than just a story with a hidden meaning, they are the great wisdom teachings of Jesus. They demand an alertness from us, speaking to our hearts through what is said, and often through what is left unsaid. Parables do not end once we are finished hearing them. They stay with us, often leaving us with unanswered questions that invite us to ponder and reflect on our own experiences; parables awaken our senses.[89]

Todays' gospel is in three parts: the parable Jesus taught, an explanation on why Jesus teaches in parables (probably added later), and an explanation of the parable of the sower (definitely added later).[90] The parable itself is well known and concerns seeds, where they land and what happens to them. We might take note of the seeds as representing God's Word and the effect it has, or does not have, on us. What makes the difference in the parable is the type of soil the seed lands on and how suitable it is for growth to take place. Let us consider our hearts the soil for a moment: how open are we to receiving seeds that may be planted there? Any decent gardener will know that good soil is key in order to cultivate anything. Soil is basically rock that has been broken down by various forces such as wind, rain, freezing and thawing. It can be too acidic, or it can be too alkaline. Good soil needs lots of air and water and some manure; it needs to be tended to and prepared. We too are weathered down by various forces in our lives, which can either close us down and harden our hearts or can open us up and help us to grow into greater awareness. How ready are our hearts for sowing? The disciple is one who hears the word and understands it, and it bears fruit.

"The soil is the great connector of lives, the source and destination of all. It is the healer and restorer and resurrector, by which disease passes into health, age into youth, death into life. Without proper care for it we can have no community, because without proper care for it we can have no life.

– Wendell Berry[91]

Go Deeper

- Consider your heart as the soil for a moment. How weathered is it? Is it open to seeds that may be planted? What might help cultivate good 'soil' of the heart?

- How do you experience the parables of Jesus? What effect have they had on your life?

16th Sunday in Ordinary Time

Matthew 13:24–43

Let it be

In today's gospel we have three 'kingdom' parables, each beginning 'The kingdom of heaven is like ...' The first of these, the parable of the weeds among the wheat, continues the theme of the different reactions to Jesus' message. When weeds are discovered among the healthy crop, the natural reaction is to extract the offending weeds. But the sower's response is clear: let them be. Leave them to grow, side by side.

The kingdom grows and spreads as it will, gradually and unpredictably. It expands outside of our judgement and our narrow ways of thinking. Society might like to separate people into categories, to judge who is valuable or not, but Jesus is clear that this is not our place: leave the field as it is. This approach lines up with the peaceful principles of the Sermon on the Mount, where Jesus calls us not to judge, to be at peace with others, to love our enemies. The parable begs the question: which am I? The grain-bearing wheat or the weeds? But for any of us, the answer is unlikely to be clearcut. Are we not a mixture of both? 'Belief and unbelief, like the wheat and the weeds in the parable, are mixed together in each one of us.'[92] There is good and bad, and everything in between, in each of us, in society and in the Church. Fortunately, Jesus allows for growth and change.

The parables of the mustard seed and the yeast, too, speak of the mysterious and hidden growth of the kingdom. These parables remind us that we don't yet fully understand; there is room for mystery. The smallest of seeds can grow into the most majestic of plants, far beyond our expectations. It is not our place to judge or to place limits on the wild and immeasurable kingdom of heaven.

" To see the world, to understand that the kingdom of heaven is like a mustard seed, requires a people who refuse to be hurried ... The kingdom of heaven is like a mustard seed or yeast because to be drawn into the kingdom of heaven is to participate in God's patience towards creation. Jesus is teaching us to see the significance of the insignificant.

– Stanley Hauerwas[93]

Go Deeper

- Jesus tells the disciples he is 'proclaiming what has been hidden'. What comes as a surprise in the parables you hear today? What new insights do they offer?

- As a Christian community, when we judge others, we shrink rather than expand the kingdom. These parables remind us that it is not our place to decide who is in or out, worthy or unworthy, but to offer the same welcome and opportunities to all, to be open to the mysterious ways of God's kingdom.

17th Sunday in Ordinary Time

Matthew 13:44–52

Hidden treasure

'Have you understood all this?' Jesus asks his disciples. Over the past few Sundays, we have heard Jesus speaking in parables to the crowds and explaining them privately to the disciples. The disciples are confident they understand everything he has said about the mysteries of the kingdom. We, the readers, are also privy to this 'insider' view. Do we understand?

The three short parables in today's gospel – comparing the kingdom of heaven to treasure, a pearl and a fishing net – are unique to Matthew's Gospel, and they are addressed only to the disciples. So what does Matthew want followers of Jesus to know about the kingdom? It is precious – so precious that its discovery requires us to put aside everything else in order to immerse ourselves wholeheartedly in it. We are called to set aside all selfishness and self-interest, all judgement, all our certainties and superior attitudes, and to live the kingdom values of humility, openness and compassion. Jesus emphasises that 'kingdom people' 'bring out of their treasure what is new and what is old'. This would have resonated with Matthew's community, a melting pot of Jews and Gentiles who were discerning the parameters of this 'new' movement.

Perhaps the fishing parable, the last in this series of parables, holds the key. It echoes the tone of the parable of the weeds among the wheat – everything is gathered in, a variety, 'good' and 'bad' alike. As he addresses his disciples, Jesus is aware that they are not perfect. Like us all, they have flaws and weaknesses. Yet we are called to this wide-open vision of Jesus, where all are gathered and none are excluded, and the hidden treasures of the kingdom are revealed.

"God's dragnet gathers all kinds. The diversity of the in-gathering is borne out in the unlikely swirl of people around Jesus: sinners and tax collectors, a Roman centurion, people with leprosy and all kinds of diseases, a Gentile woman, people possessed by demons, a little child, a disciple who betrays Jesus, a disciple who denies him, Pharisees who plot his death. All are drawn in.

– Anna Case-Winters[94]

Go Deeper

- When did you find hidden treasure? Maybe you were inspired by a powerful speaker or found peace at a retreat? Perhaps someone offered a word of wisdom that was meant just for you? We remember with gratitude the times we experienced a movement of the heart, a new treasure.

- 'Fish of every kind' are gathered in the net. All are invited and none are excluded. Reflecting on the communities you are part of, is this the case? Who has not received an invitation?

18th Sunday in Ordinary Time

Matthew 14:13–21

A kingdom feast

Today's gospel introduces us to a helpless crowd who have been following Jesus all day. They are 'running on empty' and probably wouldn't welcome the suggestion that they hike to the nearest village to buy food. Jesus feels for them. Whereas the disciples see their small offering – just five loaves and two fish – as 'nothing', he sees potential. As a result, the crowds are more than satisfied. We all have times when we're physically or emotionally exhausted and feel we have nothing left to give, whether it's time, money, energy, or even love. When we think of all the suffering in the world, we feel helpless; whatever assistance we can give will never be enough. But God sees what we have to offer, blesses and multiplies it. When we move away from an 'every person for themselves' mentality, miraculous things occur.

The humanity of Jesus in the opening verses is touching. Having learnt of the death of John the Baptist, he attempts to withdraw by himself. But the crowds, and their needs, catch up with him. Compassion takes over and he presses on with his mission, giving himself thoroughly to the people and urging the disciples to do the same: 'You give them something to eat.' No one is to be abandoned, no one left behind. This is a 'kingdom feast' in every sense. It unites past, present and future, recalling God's provision of manna in the desert (Ex 16) and foreshadowing the Last Supper (Mt 26:26–29). It is a practical provision of an inclusive and fulfilling meal, while also anticipating the heavenly or 'Messianic' feast. The kingdom values of compassion, self-giving and community shine through. Perhaps these are every bit as miraculous as the multiplication of loaves and fish.

" When I hear bread breaking, I see something else; it seems almost as though God never meant us to do anything else. So beautiful a sound, the crust breaks up like manna and falls all over everything, and then we eat.

– Daniel Berrigan[95]

Go Deeper

When Jesus heard of John's death, he wanted to be alone. It is not long before he is drawn back into community. He does not send the crowds away. Can you relate to similar experiences in your own life?

The celebration of Eucharist is a communal gathering, uniting us with God and with each other. It calls us to community where everyone is cared for and has enough for their needs. How can you respond to this call?

19th Sunday in Ordinary Time

Matthew 14:22–33

Storms ahead

Jesus has been hit by one of life's great traumas, losing John to a violent death. He makes a second attempt to withdraw from the crowds and this time succeeds in finding a place (up a mountain) to be alone and pray. He must also be reflecting on how his fate will mirror that of John. We are reminded that Jesus understands the depths of human emotions such as loss, fear and uncertainty. He is fresh from this experience when confronted with Peter's vulnerability. In the moment that Jesus calls him, Peter is all faith, stepping out of the boat in his rush to get to Jesus. This mirrors his enthusiasm and bravado elsewhere, such as when he confidently affirms 'You are the Messiah' (Mt 16:16). But as soon as he realises conditions are challenging, he starts to sink, prefiguring some of his less commendable moments, where he fails to understand (16:22) and even abandons Jesus (26:69–75). Peter, the model disciple, is a complex mix of faith and fear. The good news is that when Peter falters, Jesus reaches out to steady him and draw him close. And we hear some of his most consoling words: 'Take heart, it is I; do not be afraid.'[96]

The early readers of Matthew's Gospel were living through a period of uncertainty. The community was navigating its way through storms of insecurity and division. Our Christian community today is dealing with its own storms and divisions, fearful of losing its way. There is a narrative in the Western world that the Church is on the way out, irrelevant, sinking. Many Christians are saddened by the loss of the Church's solid place in society. Many more feel the structures of the past must be dismantled or reformed in order for a new Church to emerge. We are in need of reassurance that it is not our imperfect efforts that matter so much as the knowledge that, even in the storm, Jesus is with us, calling us to him, catching us, urging us not to be afraid, calming the storm.

> **Courage allows the successful woman to fail – and to learn powerful lessons from the failure – so that in the end, she didn't fail at all.**
>
> – Maya Angelou

Go Deeper

- In today's gospel, we can see a vulnerable side to both Peter and Jesus. Such experiences change people in different ways, perhaps making them more resilient or more compassionate. When have you found this to be true?

- Our Christian community is made up of imperfect disciples. Though we walk together towards Jesus, the storms surround us and we may lose heart. We ask Jesus to reach out his hand and encourage us to 'take heart'.

20th Sunday in Ordinary Time

Matthew 15:21–28

As you wish

Following an altercation with the religious leaders Jesus 'left that place' and went to the area of Tyre and Sidon. The geography in today's text is important because these areas were a no-go for a respectable Jew. Canaanites were despised by the people of Israel. They were exiled so that Israelites could take control of the land. Relations between these two groups were extremely hostile. By approaching Jesus, the Canaanite woman in the Gospel crosses the boundary of ethnicity as well as gender. This is a narrative on the extreme margins, in unfamiliar territory. The Canaanite woman is the first woman to speak in Matthew's Gospel. She not only speaks, she shouts at Jesus: 'Lord, help me!'

The response of Jesus that follows has disturbed biblical scholars forever. Was he joking? Was it the test of a good teacher to see how the disciples and this woman would react? We just don't know. But 'is it possible that Jesus learned from this encounter with this remarkable woman and gained a larger vision of his calling?'[97] What we do know is that this incident is of huge importance for the community that Matthew writes for as it concerns the expansion of Jesus' mission to the Gentiles. The circle is broadened from this point onward, reaching out beyond the boundaries set by the 'house of Israel'. The disciples want to 'send her away'. The woman is an inconvenience to them, and they are unable to handle her. But she will not be silenced. This brave woman claims her place at the table. This dialogue between Jesus and the woman is one that can only happen in a space of honesty and acceptance. Through her persistence she stands up for all those who are dismissed, and in doing so she is praised for her 'great faith', and her daughter is healed.

"My voice, my debate with Jesus shapes a new tradition. The release of my daughter from bondage symbolises the release of our daughters' daughters down through the ages from all that binds them, physically, socially, culturally, psychologically, racially, and religiously.

– Elaine Wainwright[98]

Go Deeper

🐚 The Canaanite woman stands to take her rightful place. What is your experience of hearing the voices of women in church? This week, check out *Catholic Women Preach*.[99]

🐚 Jesus' ministry to the 'house of Israel' is not going so well. When have experiences of rejection in your own life led to new possibilities? When have you been to an unfamiliar place and found new life?

Feast of the Assumption

Luke 1:39–56

This is my body...

The encounter we hear about in today's gospel is far from a timid rendezvous. In this narrative, we return to Mary's roots, to her early appearance as the brave, decisive, breathless, excited young woman who rushes to Elizabeth's house, pregnant with God's promise, carrying the Word of God and passing it on. Bear in mind the context, Mary is living under Roman oppression, no doubt with soldiers on street corners and people who are nervous and fearful. Yet, she is full of promise. She rejoices and finds strength in the God she finds present in Elizabeth and in her own life. Mary sets the agenda for the ministry of Jesus who 'brought down the powerful from their thrones and lifted up the lowly'.

As we celebrate the Feast of the Assumption today, remember that Mary is presented to us as the first evangelist, a prophet, a bearer of God's Word. Her entire being, flesh, bone, mind and spirit is one with God, and she rejoices. So isn't it strange that women, who know what it means to nurture and feed children from their own bodies, cannot pray the words of the Eucharistic prayer, 'This is my body', even when it was from the body of a woman that the Word became flesh? Isn't it a shame that the Church cannot say 'yes' as Mary did? Women imitate Christ every day through their lives and work; surely it is time that the visible signs of this work are now seen across all structures of the Church? 'The Church needs the ministry of women. Male and female, made in the image of God, male and female together image God.'[100]

So while we wait, let us pray the Magnificat this week, a beautiful prayer, overflowing with delight and wonder. Let us also genuinely listen to the experiences of women in our Church and in society, who in their strength and enthusiasm and despite many challenges, continue the task of carrying Christ into the world every day.

"Mary's agenda was fullness of personhood. Mary was the liberated and the liberator, Mary changed God into the body and blood of Christ; she called for miracles and got them, she made the Magnificat the national anthem of women everywhere.

– Joan Chittister[101]

Go Deeper

🐚 Pray the Magnificat this week. What great things has God done for you? You might write your own Magnificat as a spiritual exercise this week.

🐚 Mary was strong enough to know who to turn to when she needed support, not to the government, not to the synagogue, but to Elizabeth. Who are the strong women in your life? Who listens to your story? Give thanks for them. Reach out to them this week.

21st Sunday in Ordinary Time

Matthew 16:13–20

Burning question

At certain stages in life we can lose our way. A business person who starts out with a great idea can become focused only on profit and lose sight of their passion. A politician who was once idealistic becomes disillusioned. A teacher, under pressure to deliver results, loses their enthusiasm for the subject. We all have times when we get jaded, or bogged down with trivial concerns, and we forget why we do what we do. Our Christian community, too, can lose its way. The Church has not always lived up to its momentous responsibility to communicate God's love to the world.

Today's gospel encourages us to reflect on our Church and its mission. Jesus' reference to 'the keys of the kingdom of heaven' is often interpreted, in Catholic circles at least, as a reference to the origins of the Church (and the papacy). But notice what Jesus asks Peter before he hands over the metaphorical keys: 'But who do you say that I am?' This burning question gets to the heart of the Gospel. The word 'but' is crucial: Jesus is not asking the disciples what they have heard about him from others or what they understand intellectually from their time with him. He is asking them: do you really know me?

Simon Peter immediately and confidently answers, 'You are the Messiah, the Son of the living God.' Jesus responds with affirmation and renames him Peter, a play on the Greek word '*petra*', meaning rock. This brings to mind the earlier parable about those who build their houses on rock (Mt 7:24–27) representing those who not only *hear* Jesus' words but *act* on them. A thread running through Matthew's Gospel is that knowing and believing is not enough. Good intentions are not enough. Everything we do, both as individual disciples but in particular as Church, should stem from the burning question of today's gospel: 'But who do you say that I am?'

❝ Christ asks for a home in your soul, where he can be at rest with you, where he can talk easily to you, where you and he, alone together, can laugh and be silent and be delighted with one another.

– Caryll Houselander[102]

Go Deeper

- Jesus is asking us this question now: 'But who do you say that I am?' Bring this to meditation. What words flow in response to this question?
- When do you experience yourself as fully alive and life-giving? What are you passionate about?

22nd Sunday in Ordinary Time

Mt 16:21–27

Selfless love

The narrative today marks a turning point in Matthew's Gospel as we hear the first of three predictions in the Gospel concerning Jesus' death and resurrection (17:22–23; 20:17–19). Given the political climate at the time, and the fate of prophets and leaders before him, it is not a stretch to say that Jesus is fully aware of the consequences he faces. But this would be too much for the disciples, incomprehensible that the long-awaited Messiah could be crucified and die.[103] Peter is understandably upset by this thought, he probably still has notions of a political Messiah who will reign as a mighty king and overthrow the Roman occupiers. Peter has gone in a few short verses from being the 'rock', with divinely inspired insights, to being a 'stumbling block' on Jesus' path. One can also understand Jesus' frustration – the disciples still don't get it. Following Jesus means following a path that the world will not understand.

Jesus died because if you love in the way that Jesus loved and loves, the world will most certainly try to crush you. This is *agape* love, a selfless love for people regardless of who they are or their circumstances. We remember today those who have followed Jesus' path, speaking out against oppressive systems, seeking justice for those on the margins, often when it is dangerous to do so. One example is St Oscar Romero, the former archbishop of El Salvador, who was assassinated in 1980 for speaking out against the human rights violations in his country. He famously said, 'I do not believe in death without resurrection. If they kill me I will rise again in the people of El Salvador.' People like Archbishop Romero put on 'the mind of Christ', selflessly giving of themselves for their communities, pouring out love, demanding truth and justice for those who are helpless. The cross is a symbol of much suffering in our world, but it is also a symbol of liberation, because it is through that cross that restoration and healing comes. This is what Peter and the disciples and Matthew's readers will eventually learn.

> **[Jesus] crosses all boundaries and frontiers, and is occupied by only the wisdom and freedom of those who have suffered and come out the other side – not destroyed, but larger and stronger and wiser.**
>
> **– Richard Rohr[104]**

Go Deeper

- Facing moments of truth in our lives can be painful. Can you recall an experience of trying to save something and losing it? Or a time when you let go of something, only to discover a greater treasure?
- Jesus lived *agape* love, a sacrificial love, giving of himself for others. Who models this way in your community? What crosses do they bear? Who gets behind them?

❧ 7.1 ❧

The Season of Creation

Introduction to the Season of Creation (1 September–4 October)

The Season of Creation is a relatively new season in the Catholic Liturgical calendar but one which has been celebrated across many Christian churches for the past twenty-five years. As most of us are aware, we are living through a devastating environmental crisis, where the very fabric of the ecosystems of our planet is unravelling. Seventy per cent of wildlife has been destroyed in the past forty years due to human activity. The continuing rise in toxic greenhouse gas emissions is fuelling a climate crisis that is making parts of our world uninhabitable for human beings. It is the world's poorest who are suffering the most now, and it will be even worse for future generations. What is most disturbing is that the scientists are sounding the alarm bells loud and clear, yet the world is not responding with the urgency that is needed. Pope Francis describes the roots of the environmental crisis as deeply spiritual, therefore faith communities have a clear role to play in inspiring an ecological conversion amongst believers.

And so, within Ordinary Time, the Season of Creation gives us an opportunity to come together to renew our relationship with God's creation. It runs from the World Day of Prayer for Creation on 1 September to the Feast of St Francis of Assisi on 4 October. It has its origins in the Orthodox Church, which in 1989 proclaimed 1 September as a day of prayer for creation. Subsequently, the World Council of Churches extended the celebration until 4 October. Many Christians around the world embraced this idea, and in 2015 Pope Francis officially declared 1 September the World Day of Prayer for Creation in the Catholic calendar. This means that the world's 2.2 billion Christians now celebrate the Season of Creation as an ecumenical occasion worldwide.

In 2015 Pope Francis published his ground-breaking encyclical on the environment, *Laudato Si': On Care for Our Common Home*. In it he calls on all people of the world to enter into dialogue about what is happening to our planet, urging us to listen to both the cry of the earth and the cry of the poor. He invites us to 'become painfully aware' of the extent of this crisis and to engage in the conversion that is needed to protect our common home. In light of the urgent ecological crisis our world is facing and the addition of the Season of Creation to our liturgical calendar, the reflections for the next five Sundays will focus on this theme, as well as paying attention to the gospel of the day. All Christians are invited to embrace this season wholeheartedly, through deep reflection, through living more sustainably, through raising our voices in the public sphere and in a special way through our liturgies.

We are invited to think more deeply about what is happening to the earth right now, to recognise the environmental destruction that now threatens our world, to accept the call to 'eco-conversion' and as faith communities to lead by example in living out our vocation to care for God's creation, our common home (cf. Gen 2:15).

Lectio Divina with Nature[105]

In *Laudato Si'* we read that 'Saint Francis, faithful to Scripture, invites us to see nature as a magnificent book in which God speaks to us and grants us a glimpse of his infinite beauty and goodness' (*Laudato Si'*, 12). It is a reminder to us that while we encounter God in the Book of the Word, we also encounter God in the Book of Nature. The practice of *Lectio Divina with Nature* might seem strange to us, but it is a practice rooted in the mystical tradition of the Church and most notably in the life of St Francis of Assisi. No doubt, since human beings have walked on this earth, we have been contemplating God's presence in nature. We see this most notably in the Psalms:

O Lord, how manifold are your works!
In wisdom you have made them all;
the earth is full of your creatures. (Psalm 104:24)

At various times throughout the Year of Matthew and especially during this Season of Creation, we suggest this practice of *Lectio Divina with Nature* so that we may hear God's Word as spoken to us through creation, in order to love God more deeply (Rom 1:19–20).[106] We enter into a deeper relationship with God and embrace the one who calls us out of darkness and into her own wonderful light. We may find that this in turn rekindles in us a sense of awe and wonder for our world and a desire to care more deeply for our common home. We are called at this moment in history to listen to the cry of the earth, to hear what God is saying to us now through the Book of Creation.

Look at the birds of the air ... Consider the lilies of the field ...
(Mt 6:26–28)

- *Lectio* (Reading): When we read a story, we attend to the words, characters, places and things that unfold. When we read nature, we attend to the elements by going outside on a walk, sitting in a garden, or even in your own home with a plant. Take time to 'read' creation by just walking or looking around, slowly taking in what is around you. At first, sense the overview rather than the details. Then, begin to notice the different colours, shapes, smells, textures. Evoke the senses. What do you see, hear, touch, smell? Notice if something attracts your attention, and when that happens allow yourself to linger there, taking more time to savour this

134

particular element. What plant or leaf captivates you? What colour or scent or shape draws you in? Allow yourself to be present to what is there. Embrace wonder and fascination with this element of creation. Notice any word or feeling that comes up for you, without analysing it.

- *Meditatio* (Reflecting): Take this word or feeling into deeper contemplation. Imagine the process that led to this plant or creature's existence; again sense the overview of the wider ecosystem. Become aware of yourself not as an observer but as a participant, deeply embedded in this web of life. Listen attentively. Be open to what God is saying to you through creation.

- *Oratio* (Prayer): We are moved to respond to God's presence in creation: in nature, in flora, fauna or in the elements themselves, the way the air is, the way the water is, the light, the sea, the surf, the sky, a cloud. Speak to God, perhaps giving thanks for the beauty of this creation, then allow yourself to listen. After some time, words and thoughts melt away. Allow yourself to rest in God's presence.

When you are ready to close your time of prayer, find a way to give thanks: silently offer a prayer of gratitude, make a gesture of gratitude (the sign of the cross, a deep bow). You might say, 'May all beings be well; May all beings be free from harm; May all beings live in peace and harmony.'

The entire material universe speaks of God's love, his boundless affection for us. Soil, water, mountains, everything is as it were, a caress of God (*Laudato Si'*, 84).

23rd Sunday in Ordinary Time / Season of Creation 1

Matthew 18:15–20

Our common home

Matthew chapter 18 is concerned with how the early Christian community might live together in harmony. It reminds us that the Church should be a place where the least are considered the greatest and the last first, where we look out for the most vulnerable, where we are accountable to one another and forgive each other. In today's text, Jesus sets out a vision for his followers concerning disputes within the community. The process he lays out is a respectful one, and it is also realistic, because some people will not respond to this advice.[107] The teaching reminds us that as Church, we belong to one another, sisters and brothers, one body (1 Cor 12).

As we enter the beautiful Season of Creation, this is an appropriate text, for it invites us to reflect on how we are called to live in harmony. The realities of the ecological crises our world faces today highlight the great *disharmony* that exists between humanity and God's creation. We are not living in right relationship with the natural world nor with our sisters and brothers who are suffering the most from the climate and biodiversity crises. We are not living in right relationship with young people who are now growing up for 'we may well be leaving to coming generations, debris, desolation and filth' (*Laudato Si'*, 161). Pope Francis calls the destruction of nature an ecological sin.[108] This is not easy to hear, for it makes demands on us. The good news is that there is a cure. *Laudato Si'* calls us to a profound interior conversion where our relationship with nature is concerned. Today's gospel reminds us that there are moments when we must speak the truth in love for the greater good. The Season of Creation presents us with such a moment, where we can create awareness across our communities so that together we can discern how to care more deeply for God's creation. For this is our common home, the home we all share. We are not alone, Christ is with us on this journey: 'For where two or three are gathered in my name, I am there among them'.

> **"The climate crisis is a deeply spiritual crisis ... Our faith offers us a wonderful vision to rekindle these relationships, to renew a childlike sense of awe, wonder and beauty and thus set out in living the first commandment God gave to us, to be guardians and protectors of this beautiful world, not its polluters and destroyers.**
> **– Archbishop Dermot Farrell[109]**

Go Deeper

Ecological conversion involves a profound movement of the heart where our relationship with God's creation is concerned. This week, spend more time in nature in deeper awareness of the beauty of our world. See *Lectio Divina with Nature* on page 133.

24th Sunday in Ordinary Time / Season of Creation 2

Matthew 18:21–35

Turning around

We continue to read from Matthew 18 on the virtues that are essential for the Christian community, and today's parable deals with forgiveness. Peter is told to forgive seventy times seven, a number which represents infinity, that is, endless forgiveness. God's grace and mercy is abundant, and we are called to extend that grace and mercy to others. The vision which is unfolding in Matthew's Gospel emphasises restoring relationships and wholeness within the community and this usually involves a change in perspective. As Christian communities today, we are certainly faced with a new question: what does restoration and wholeness look like in an era of ecological breakdown?

During this Season of Creation can we admit to ourselves that our relationship with God's creation is fractured? Coming into this awareness is a painful process. It means awakening to the realities of the loss of biodiversity, the fact that we are spewing millions of tons of harmful greenhouse gases into the thin shell of our atmosphere, the destruction of our great forests, the pollution of our oceans and rivers with plastic, the degradation of the soil and wetlands, our 'throwaway culture'. All of these things cause us great distress, and we feel it on a level that we are not even aware of. Our *turning around* begins by sitting in this painful awareness of what is and, like the slaves in the parable today who 'saw what had happened' and 'were greatly distressed', we are called to respond to what we see. Beginning to *see* the need for reconciliation with God, with our sisters and brothers who are suffering, and with creation which cries out to us is the first step on this journey of ecological conversion. 'For we know that things can change' (*Laudato Si'*, 13).

138

Go Deeper

The Ignatian Ecological Examen[110] is a wonderful (and challenging) tool to help us discern a way forward. Find a quiet place this week and see if these questions aid reflection:

- Begin in gratitude: giving thanks to God for creation. Notice where you felt God's presence in creation today.

- Come into awareness: ask for the grace to see creation as God does – in all its splendour and in all its suffering. Do you see the beauty of creation and hear the cry of the earth and the poor?

- Ask for the gift of conversion: where have I fallen short in caring for creation? Ask for the grace of a conversion of the heart.

- Reconciliation: how might I reconcile this relationship with God, creation and humanity? Can I stand in solidarity through my actions and make choices consistent with my desire for reconciliation with creation?

- Offer a closing prayer for the earth and those now suffering the effects of climate change and biodiversity loss.

25th Sunday in Ordinary Time / Season of Creation 3

Matthew 20:1–16

Unequal opportunities

The parables of Jesus challenge our certainties about the world. Today, we hear the story of the landowner who pays the same wages to all his workers. Although they receive the promised wage, the 'early birds' feel hard done by. Perhaps we can relate. Our individualistic culture tells us that only some people deserve a decent standard of living. But this narrative ignores the reality that people do not have equal opportunities or privileges in life. In this Season of Creation, we are mindful in particular of those who suffer as a result of environmental damage caused by the comfortable lifestyles of others. One example of this is the palm oil industry. A popular ingredient in foods and cosmetic products, the production of palm oil contributes to the large-scale destruction of tropical forests, loss of habitat for endangered species, soil erosion and loss of livelihood.

Earth is our common home. Like the labourers, every person on Earth deserves equal dignity and the means to flourish. It is deeply unjust that a large percentage of the world's population suffers from poverty, simply by virtue of being born in a particular place. In today's parable, Jesus subverts expectations: everyone is to be treated equally, regardless of their opportunities or productivity. Instead of self-interest, we are called to deep concern for the common good. Jesus concludes with the refrain: 'the last will be first, and the first will be last'. Not only is there no discrimination in the kingdom, but we are to go beyond what might appear fair and give preferential treatment to those who are without privilege. In *Laudato Si'*, Pope Francis summons us to a 'preferential option for the poor'[III], referring to a trend throughout the Scriptures of God siding with the most vulnerable and powerless people.

Solidarity with the world's poorest involves an honest examination of our attitudes and lifestyles, making choices that propel us forward into a world where 'the last will be first'.

> **The rejection of every form of self-centeredness and self-absorption are essential if we truly wish to care for our brothers and sisters and for the natural environment. These attitudes also attune us to the moral imperative of assessing the impact of our every action and personal decision on the world around us.**
>
> *– Pope Francis*[112]

Go Deeper

- What uncomfortable truths emerge for you in this parable? To see the world as Jesus does requires an adjustment in attitude, an awareness that everyone matters equally.

- The choices consumers make can support others or perpetuate unjust systems, build up or tear down. Focus this week on researching some of the products you use. For example, which ones contain palm oil, and where does it come from?[113]

26th Sunday in Ordinary Time /
Season of Creation 4

Matthew 21:28–32

Walking the talk

Jesus and the disciples have entered Jerusalem and the conflict that has been building with the religious leaders is reaching its climax. Jesus has cleared the moneychangers out of the Temple, healed people inside the Temple, the children are crying out 'hosanna to the Son of David', and this chaotic scene is just all too much for the chief priests. Who does this guy think he is? Then, Jesus teaches the parable of the two sons, which is a lesson for the religious leaders against hypocrisy. This parable, unique to Matthew, reaffirms a great upheaval; those considered to be on the fringes of society are the ones who respond to Jesus' message,[114] yet those who say the right thing do not walk the talk.

In *Laudato Si'* Pope Francis criticises the failure of global summits to take the urgent action that is needed on the environmental crisis. He says, 'recent World Summits on the environment have not lived up to expectations because, due to lack of political will, they were unable to reach truly meaningful and effective global agreements on the environment.' (*Laudato Si'*, 166). He notes that this is due to positions taken by countries which place national interests and infinite economic growth above the global common good (*Laudato Si'*, 169). This is in spite of devastating climate and biodiversity disasters worldwide and annual UN scientific reports that continue to sound the alarm bells and call our present situation a 'code red for humanity'.[115]

While world leaders are not walking the talk, it is clear that there is a swelling of grassroots activists who speak truth to power and who are taking action on the environmental crisis in their own backyards and local communities. One such person is Dr Rajwant Singh, who founded Eco-Sikh, an organisation in India aiming to plant one million trees by 2030. They are already half way to their target simply by asking each Sikh community in their region to plant 550 trees per community, a very doable task. Millions of people around the world are walking the talk at the grassroots, helping to heal our common home, cleansing this Temple. With over 220,000 Catholic parishes in the world, imagine what we could achieve if each parish community put their mind to it.

> 66 **Jesus Christ did not wait for the Roman Emperor, he just got on with it. So, let's just get on with it.**
>
> – Dr Rajwant Singh[116]

Go Deeper

This week do one small thing: plant a native tree, wildflower an area (the church or a graveyard or parish land could be a longer-term project), say goodbye to single-use plastics, ask your local eco-groups for advice on what is happening where you are and how you can contribute.

27th Sunday in Ordinary Time /
Season of Creation 5

Matthew 21:33–43

The fruits of the kingdom

Jesus is in the Temple, addressing the chief priests and elders who are questioning his authority. With his parable of the wicked tenants, he issues a rebuke and a challenge to these religious leaders who believe they alone have authority. The tenants in the parable are not fulfilling their responsibilities: instead of tending the vineyard entrusted to them, they are only looking after themselves. If we think of the vineyard as our world, this parable jumps into the modern age. Humanity has been entrusted with this beautiful and bountiful world, but instead of caring for it and sharing its fruits, those in power exploit it for their own benefit. The parable is critical of the entitled attitude of those who take, but refuse to offer anything in return. Jesus ends with a warning that the precious vineyard will be leased to better tenants – 'a people that produces the fruits of the kingdom'. We've heard this language before in the Beatitudes, when Jesus says the kingdom belongs to the meek, pure in heart, just, merciful. These are the carers our earth needs.

Sr Dorothy Stang was a missionary in Brazil where she dedicated her ministry to farmers and was an outspoken critic of illegal logging in the Amazonian region. Frustrated at the destruction of the rainforest for financial gain, Sr Dorothy campaigned tirelessly for the protection of the people and natural resources of the region. This made her a target among the power brokers of the area. On 2 February 2005, two hired gunmen fired six shots and killed Sr Dorothy as she was walking on a rural road. As her killers approached, she took out her Bible and began to read from the Beatitudes: 'Blessed are those who hunger and thirst for righteousness...' Following Sr Dorothy's death, the Brazilian president placed 20,000 square miles of the

Amazon under federal environmental protection. The dream of this brave woman lives on, even though illegal logging continues elsewhere in Brazil and other places today. Sr Dorothy was a kingdom person, a 'tenant' dedicated to preserving the Earth for the good of all.

> **We can no longer let the people in power decide what is politically possible. We can no longer let the people in power decide what hope is. Hope is not passive. Hope is telling the truth. Hope is taking action. And hope always comes from the people.**
>
> – Greta Thunberg[117]

Go Deeper

We are called to care for this precious vineyard, Earth, our common home. This involves spiritual conversion and action. To help discern our response, Pope Francis has launched seven *Laudato Si'* goals for us to try and achieve by 2030. This week, visit the online *Laudato Si'* Action Platform and consider enrolling as a family or community.[118]

Season of Creation 6 / Feast of St Francis of Assisi

4 October

Living in harmony

We mark the end of the Season of Creation by celebrating the Feast of St Francis of Assisi. St Francis and his friars were street preachers. As they moved around, they were expected to 'live lightly on the earth, a burden neither to the earth nor to those who met their sustenance needs'.[119] St Francis lived in harmony with creation, with a sense of wonder and praise for God's gift of life and the gift of creation.

St Francis, the patron saint of ecology, was someone who came from a life of privilege but embraced a life of Christ-like poverty. As well as helping the poor and sick, he cared deeply about all creatures on Earth, often preaching about animals and calling them 'brother' and 'sister' and inviting flowers to 'praise the Lord'. This language is part of his famous prayer, the 'Canticle of the Sun', which refers to Brother Sun, Sister Moon, Brother Wind, Sister Water, Brother Fire, Mother Earth.[120] St Francis embraces a deep integral ecology, aware of just how deeply interconnected everything is . He shows us that care for creation is inseparable from justice for the poor and interior peace. He lived out this integral ecology joyfully, with an open heart.

St Francis takes us to the heart of what it is to be human and invites us to profound interior conversion. He challenges us to 'see nature as a magnificent book in which God speaks to us and grants us a glimpse of his infinite beauty and goodness' (*Laudato Si'*, 12).

We are called into this awareness so that we can begin to repair our broken relationship with the natural world, turn away from destruction and, feeling intimately connected to all that exists, care more deeply for our common home. The natural beauty and diversity of our planet call us into a deeper communion with the Earth and with God.

> **"**If we approach nature and the environment without this openness to awe and wonder, if we no longer speak the language of fraternity and beauty in our relationship with the world, our attitude will be that of masters, consumers, ruthless exploiters, unable to set limits on their immediate needs. By contrast, if we feel intimately united with all that exists, then sobriety and care will well up spontaneously.

> – *Pope Francis*[121]

Go Deeper

- To mark the feast of St Francis, residents of Assisi light lamps to remember the saint, while others undertake voluntary activities to help the poor. Many parishes hold services to bless household pets. How can your community celebrate St Francis?

- Look back on the Season of Creation and gather the fruits. What was your experience? What new insights did you come to? Where are you being called to act?

28th Sunday in Ordinary Time

Matthew 22:1–14

Invite everyone you find

The parable we hear today is the third of three parables that Jesus aims at the chief priests and the elders about the kingdom of heaven. Jesus compares the kingdom of heaven to a great wedding banquet and this is symbolic of God's relationship with God's people. When invitations to this feast are rejected, we are told that the king sends troops to destroy the city. It's a rather fierce reaction when we consider the king to represent God. The context here is important as Matthew's community would have been trying to make sense of the destruction of Jerusalem by the Romans (AD 70) including the destruction of the Jerusalem Temple, the holiest of places in Judaism. Some probably saw it as punishment from God for Jesus' death. The judgments sound harsh, but the criticism here is directed at some of the religious leaders and how they have interpreted the law for ordinary people, often in extremely oppressive ways. If God is portrayed as a tyrant in this parable, it is because some of the religious elite have inflicted this image of God on the people. If the parable challenges us to do anything, it is to critique certain interpretations of how God operates in our world. In Jesus' teaching, the kingdom is opened wide and new guests are invited from the 'main streets'; he says, 'invite everyone you find'. The invitation to this banquet is not restricted to the social elite and powerful; it is wide open to those considered unwanted and the hall is 'filled with guests'.

Matthew's addition to this parable about the wedding robe seems harsh; how could this poor man be expected to find wedding robes at such short notice? There was a tradition in the early Christian community that 'putting on' a new robe was symbolic of a new way of life, 'clothe yourselves with compassion, kindness, humility, meekness and patience ... clothe yourselves with love, which binds everything together in perfect harmony' (Col 3:12, 14).[122] These are the attitudes that the Christian community are to wear so that everyone can attend this mighty feast.

> **" The church is not a select circle of the immaculate, but a home where the outcast may come in... a hospital where the broken-hearted may be healed, and where all the weary and troubled may find rest.**
>
> **– James H. Aughey**

Go Deeper

🐚 Many situations in our world reflect the exclusion of people from the banquet. During the COVID-19 pandemic, pharmaceutical companies refused to waiver patents for vaccines, favouring profits instead. This meant that people in poorer countries could not access vaccines. What other situations of injustice come to mind when we think of how people are excluded in our world? How do we widen the invitation?

29th Sunday in Ordinary Time

Matthew 22:15–21

What bears God's image

In the first of three 'conflict stories', we read today that the Pharisees are looking to Jesus for advice on their taxes. They try to flatter him first, ironically by speaking the truth about him, but the tone is still disrespectful. This is a dangerous situation because in an unlikely alliance, the Pharisees have brought along the Herodians with them. The Herodians were great supporters of the Roman Empire, so tensions here would have been high. If Jesus answers 'no' to their question about paying taxes to Caesar he risks being reported to the Roman authorities as a revolutionary; if he says 'yes' then he may be accused of colluding with the occupying Empire and abandoning the people. Jesus sees through this 'malice' and speaks truth to power. He invites us to explore another way, a third way, one that is not a revolt but neither does it lie down and submit to oppression. Yes, do your civic duty, but do not forget what belongs to God; this overrides any political power. This is how one truly advocates for the kingdom of heaven in the here and now.

In 2018 and again in 2019, Pope Francis met the CEOs of the world's major fossil fuel companies at the Vatican.[123] He reminded them that today's ecological crisis threatens the very future of the human family and our common home. He told them that 'a radical energy transition was needed to save our common home' and that while 'civilisation requires energy ... energy use must not destroy civilisation.'[124] Pope Francis is not afraid to speak truth to power, urging these powerful corporations to go beyond merely exploring what needs to be done and actually concentrating on what needs to be done. Embarking on this new path will generate new jobs, reduce inequality and improve the quality of life for all. Being a follower of Jesus means that we prioritise the values that Jesus teaches so that we can be co-creators of this wild and wonderful kingdom of heaven here on earth.

> **" There is no time to lose: We received the earth as a garden-home from the Creator; let us not pass it on to future generations as a wilderness.**
>
> – *Pope Francis*[125]

Go Deeper

- Sometimes kingdom values come into conflict with the status quo. When have you experienced this? How were you called to respond?

- We have the ability to change the way businesses and governments operate, for example, by moving away from products with excess packaging, finding out if your bank, university, diocese or insurance company have divested from the fossil fuel industry, supporting the Youth Climate Movement who are persuading governments to change course. What else comes to mind?

30th Sunday in Ordinary Time

Matthew 22:34–40

The lens of love

The religious elite continue their attempts to discredit Jesus as he teaches in the Temple; they try to trick him by asking which of the laws of Judaism are the most important. Jesus responds by quoting Deuteronomy 6:5 and Leviticus 19:18: 'love the Lord your God ... love your neighbour as yourself'. All other laws 'hang' on these two; they are the lens through which all else is to be interpreted. This Wisdom saying can sometimes be dismissed as sentimentality, but here Jesus is speaking a deep truth. Both commandments are interconnected, 'like' one another, and their foundation is to love God with our entire being, 'heart ... soul and ... mind'. That means sitting with the truth that God is love and dwells within each person; this is our true self (1 Cor 3:16). This brings the question, can we cope with this? Are we able to open our hearts in awareness to this love, to tap into this divine indwelling? Then we can truly love our neighbour as ourselves – not *as much* as ourselves, but as a complete continuation of our very being. Thomas Keating once said, 'We're all like localised vibrations of the infinite goodness of God's presence. So love is our very nature. Love is our first, middle, and last name.'[126]

In Matthew chapter 18 we read what this love of neighbour involves: bringing restoration to the community, solving disputes, forgiving one another ... serving others. This is a lifelong task, and we cannot do it alone. Cultivating a deep awareness of the Source of this love that dwells within, in turn allows this love to flow outward. This love invites us to open our hearts fully to the Divine, to reject individualism and embrace a radical solidarity with our fellow human beings and with all of creation. The religious leaders dare not ask Jesus any more questions (22:46); they have been 'amazed' (v. 22), 'astounded' (v. 33) and 'silenced' (v. 34).

" How do we put on the mind of Christ? How do we see through his eyes? How do we feel through his heart? How do we learn to respond to the world with that same wholeness and healing love? That's what Christian orthodoxy is all about. It's not about right belief; it's about right practice.

– Cynthia Bourgeault[127]

Go Deeper

🐦 Can you sit with an awareness of the Divine who dwells within? This week, in contemplation, bring your awareness to the heart centre, and Christ seated there in compassion and love. You might use a mantra to help you: 'My Lord and my God' or 'Íosa', 'Jesu'.

🐦 What does the outpouring of this 'love your neighbour' look like in a world ravaged by environmental destruction, conflict, loneliness? Bring this to prayer.

31st Sunday in Ordinary Time

Matthew 23:1–12

Wake-up call

We are familiar with the expression, 'Do as I say, not as I do.' According to one definition, it is 'an expression used to call out hypocrites, including "environmentalists" with private jets, politicians who send their children to private school while opposing measures to give other kids the same chance, or those who accuse others of racism while not hiring minorities.'[128] Another example is politicians who publicly advocated social distancing and mask wearing during the COVID-19 pandemic while doing the opposite in private gatherings. Jesus makes a similar accusation about the scribes and Pharisees: 'do whatever they teach you and follow it; but do not do as they do'. He criticises them for placing heavy burdens on people and for making themselves look important in order to attract attention.

The Pharisees were part of a reform movement concerned with the laws of purity, piety and Sabbath observance. They were well-intentioned, wishing to cement Jewish identity in the face of surrounding cultures and threats. It is easy today to denounce the abuses that Jesus highlights here and place ourselves at the opposite end of the spectrum. But if we take the opportunity to examine our own lives and faith practice, how might we fare? If we are overly concerned with religious duties and displays of piety, we miss the call to humility and service. How would our Church stand up to the criticisms of Jesus? Jesus' vision is of a community that is sincere, egalitarian and humble. It is a community that learns and grows: 'you are all students', he reminds them. The use of titles such as 'rabbi', 'father' and 'instructor' remove the focus from God and lure their holders into a sense of superiority that is damaging to the community. Again, we have a topsy-turvy saying of Jesus to drive home the point: 'All who exalt themselves will be humbled, and all who humble themselves will be exalted.' These are strong words, and a wake-up call for the Christian community.

"My abiding concern is about the loss of the reassuring invitation of a beckoning God, as revealed so unambiguously in the life of Jesus. Jesus was so good at simply walking with people without judging them, liberating people without making them dependent, forgiving people unconditionally while saving their embarrassment. He set out only to bless people with their own divine power.

– Daniel O'Leary[129]

Go Deeper

- Today's gospel makes uncomfortable reading for those in positions of leadership. What are the signs of a good leader? Who models genuine leadership in your community?

- Jesus calls each one of us to service, to lift burdens from people rather than make life more difficult. How can I live this call to service in my family, my friendships, my work, my community?

Feast of All Saints

Matthew 5:1–12

What makes a saint?

In 1987, Dr Paul Farmer founded Partners in Health in Haiti. Its mission was to provide high-quality healthcare to patients from impoverished backgrounds and those who lived far from healthcare facilities. Over the following thirty years, the organisation expanded across Africa, Latin America, Russia and the Navajo Nation in the US. Dr Farmer's goal was to make the latest sophisticated treatments, which were available only in wealthy regions, available to all people. He was instrumental in bringing lifesaving HIV drugs to the people of Haiti in the early 2000s and was later involved in founding a medical school in Rwanda, where he had been teaching before he passed away unexpectedly in February 2022. Described as a 'global health champion', Dr Farmer's driving forces were equality, solidarity and love. His central philosophy could be summed up in his own words: 'The idea that some lives matter less is the root of all that is wrong with the world.' Dr Farmer was a social justice campaigner, what some might call a modern saint. Aware of the disparities around the world, he set about finding creative ways to narrow the gap.

Saints are all around us, teaching us about God through their actions. They persevere in all they do for their communities and those on the margins. They are the blessed ones. The Paul Farmers of this world inspire us to strive to live the Beatitudes of Jesus in our daily lives. The Beatitudes are an urgent call to honour the dignity of all people, especially those who suffer. The most pressing need of our time is to bridge the gap between the haves and the have-nots. When we hear of the disparity between the incomes and lifestyles of the super-rich and the poorest people in the world, it can be hard to stomach. Becoming aware of our privilege is the first step towards solidarity. The Beatitudes call us to put our hunger for justice into action. Perhaps that is the making of all saints.

"[Saints] make our hypocrisy so apparent that we want to change our lives – not because of guilt but because we want to be alive, we want to be more like Jesus...[they] leave us the scent of God, the aroma of Christ. God occasionally drops a handkerchief – and these handkerchiefs are called saints.

– Shane Claiborne[130]

Go Deeper

- Think about your immediate local community. What inequalities do you notice? Which individuals or groups are treated as if their lives matter less than others?

- Sometimes special 'saints' come into your life, teaching you about the kind of person you would like to be. Who has had that impact on you? What qualities did they espouse?

32nd Sunday in Ordinary Time

Matthew 25:1–13

Keep the lamps lit

As we approach the end of the Church year the gospel for the next few Sundays turn their focus to talk of end times. The early Christians expected Jesus to return quite quickly and Matthew's community must have been wondering what was taking so long. So, as Matthew prepares them for a long wait, these parables are all concerned with how the Christian community should live in the meantime.

This parable of the bridesmaids is unique to Matthew. In first-century Palestine it was custom for the bridegroom to be escorted to the home of the bride by the bridesmaids. Then the bridesmaids would escort the couple to the house where the wedding and the party would take place. We hear of the different levels of preparedness of the bridesmaids, those who took extra oil for the lamps and those who 'took no oil with them'.[131] We can speculate as to what the oil in the lamps represents, and perhaps it is different for each of us: the inner wisdom we know we should trust but are afraid to, that deep awareness of God's indwelling presence, a sense of fulfilment that we experience from doing acts of justice and mercy (5:20; 7:21–27), loving God and neighbour (22:37–38). The 'foolish' were lacking in evidence of such deeds and so, the Lord does not know them. But to hear that they were then 'shut out' is horrifying; the disappointment, anxiety and regret can be felt off the page.

Sometimes, we too find ourselves in this 'foolish' position, and when that happens the challenge is not to let ourselves close down. It is during such times we have the opportunity for conversion and through that the grace of gaining some insight or wisdom. We learn much from these experiences, unpleasant though they may be. If this parable leaves us confused, appalled, with tons of questions, even a bit shaken, then, good! This is the parable doing its thing. Jesus was certainly not a boring teacher and at this stage of the Gospel, as he is about to be arrested, it is not surprising that he is warning those around him to have enough oil for their lamps.

> **"Wisdom is radiant and unfading, and she is easily discerned by those who love her, and is found by those who seek her.**
>
> **– Wisdom 6:12**

Go Deeper

- There are times in life when we find ourselves in similar positions to the 'wise' and 'foolish' bridesmaids; we can identify with both. Looking back on these times can you recognise the grace that was there? What was revealed to you? How did you grow?

- What might the oil in the lamp represent for you? How can you ensure a steady supply?

33rd Sunday in Ordinary Time

Matthew 25:14–30

Enter into joy

The slaves in today's parable have been entrusted with their master's property, 'each according to his ability'. The 'talent' was an unreal sum of money to be responsible for as one 'talent' was equivalent to fifteen years' wages. The slaves are not all expected to have the same outcomes, but their master does expect some progress.[132] While the first two slaves make great returns, the third slave buries his talent. This was one way of keeping money safe in the ancient world (13:44), but it also removed liability from the person who buried it. This poor slave is afraid of failure and appears a bit lazy, he does nothing with his talent and so loses everything. While the word 'talent' comes from this very parable, it is about more than our gifts. It points towards a bigger picture: how will Jesus' followers *be* in this world following his death?

We have no idea when the 'end times' will come, but we do know that each of us has a limited amount of time at our disposal; we will all, eventually, run out of time! The parable asks Matthew's community, and us, how we might live responsibly, using the opportunities that are given to us for the good of the world and the glory of God. Digging a hole and hiding our gifts, and in doing so hiding ourselves, is certainly not the way to go. Everything is moving towards fulfilment, our very lives and all of creation. So the challenge put before us here is, what will we do with the time that has been given to us? The parable encourages us to use our time and gifts creatively, embracing adventure, being curious about what possibilities might come if we take a chance. Jesus calls us to the fullness of life so that we can *enter into joy*.

> "It is our light, not our darkness that most frightens us. We ask ourselves, Who am I to be brilliant, gorgeous, talented, and fabulous? Actually, who are you not to be? You are a child of God. Your playing small does not serve the world. There is nothing enlightened about shrinking... We were born to make manifest the glory of God that is within us.
>
> – Marianne Williamson[133]

Go Deeper

- People who have no faith in themselves or motivation, like the third slave, lose what they have been given. Sometimes a mentor comes to their aid. Where have you seen this happening?
- Joy is more than happiness. It is deep-rooted, grace-filled, inspiring and brings satisfaction. What is your experience of joy? Celebrate joy this week.

Feast of Christ the King /
Last Sunday in Ordinary Time

Matthew 25:31–46

Namaste

We have arrived at the final Sunday in the liturgical calendar and this Feast of Christ the King brings our journey with Matthew's Gospel to a close, for now. Instead of palaces or trappings, today we have Christ the King found dwelling with those who are on the fringes of society: prisoners, the hungry, the naked. How transformative it would be to really see God present in each other and in those that society considers the 'least'. There is a beautiful practice in India of using the phrase 'Namaste' when you greet someone, which literally means, the Divine in me greets the Divine in you. Usually this greeting is accompanied by a deep bow towards the other person. Words are one thing, but can we live this? At the heart of the mystery of today's gospel is the radical call to *be* Christ to others and to *see* Christ in others.

Acts of love, mercy and compassion towards the 'least' in the community are a summary of Jesus' ministry in Matthew's Gospel, keys to the kingdom of heaven.[134] Jesus is never afraid to call out good and evil, and while this might make us uncomfortable, it presents us with the opportunity to go deeper, to recognise the weeds and the wheat, the sheep and the goats in our world but also within ourselves. We are called to him by giving our lives in service to those around, recognising Christ in those we meet and within ourselves. All are sacred. This is 'good news', even the righteous in the parable today are surprised to be recognised (v. 37). The call is to contemplative action, and there should be no half measure as we have seen in the previous parables: stay alert, use our gifts and talents, keep the lamps lit.

To really live this, to love God who dwells within, through loving our neighbour who is Christ to us, is to be true to the greatest commandment.

> **“**We need not worry about the timing of the 'second coming'. Christ is in our midst now and comes to us again and again – unexpectedly – in the form of the person in need.
>
> – Anna Case-Winters[135]

Go Deeper

- We meet Christ in the simple gestures: feeding the hungry, visiting the sick, clothing the naked, visiting the prisoner. We also meet Christ in ourselves: for what do you hunger and thirst? What needs welcoming in you?

- Our journey through Matthew ends here with an invitation to see Christ in every person we meet and through acts of compassion and mercy birthing transformative grace into the world. May we live the Gospel with our lives.

Index of Scripture References

Genesis 1:2 94
Genesis 2:7 171
Genesis 2:15 133
Genesis 15:12–21 168
Genesis 28:10–22 168
Genesis 37 168
Genesis 40–41 168
Exodus 16 120
Leviticus 19:17 174
Leviticus 19:18 152
Leviticus 25 30
Deuteronomy 6:5 152
1 Samuel 3:3–14 168
2 Kings 1:8 168
Psalms 104:24 134
Isaiah 9:1–2 169
Isaiah 61 30
Ezekiel 37:5 171
Hosea 6:6 104
Wisdom 6:12 159

Matthew 1–2 167
Matthew 1:1–17 .... 17, 19
Matthew 1:18–20 18
Matthew 1:18–24 32
Matthew 1:20–21 .... 18, 168, 173
Matthew 1:22 167
Matthew 1:23 .... 18, 92
Matthew 2:6 18
Matthew 2:1–12 .... 44, 174

Matthew 2:12 168
Matthew 2:13–22 168
Matthew 2:13–15, 19–23 40
Matthew 2:15, 23 167
Matthew 3:1–12 26
Matthew 3:2 30
Matthew 3:3 46
Matthew 3:13–17 46
Matthew 4:1–11 64
Matthew 4:12–23 52
Matthew 4:14–16 167
Matthew 4:15 92
Matthew 5–7 .... 19, 102
Matthew 5:1–12 .... 54, 156
Matthew 5:7 12
Matthew 5:13–16 56
Matthew 5:17–20 .... 17, 18
Matthew 5:20 158
Matthew 5:17–37 58
Matthew 5:21–48 32
Matthew 5:38–48 60
Matthew 6:24–34 100
Matthew 6:26–28 134
Matthew 7:21–27 .... 102, 158
Matthew 7:24–27 128
Matthew 7:29 92
Matthew 8:5–13 174
Matthew 8:17 167
Matthew 8:26 173
Matthew 9:9 16

Matthew 9:9–13 104
Matthew 9:20–22 19
Matthew 9:36 18
Matthew 9:36–10:8 106
Matthew 10:1 92
Matthew 10:3 16
Matthew 10:6 18
Matthew 10:7 52
Matthew 10:26–33 108
Matthew 10:31 173
Matthew 10:37–42 110
Matthew 11:2–11 30
Matthew 11:5 176
Matthew 11:25–30 ...... 18, 112, 173
Matthew 12:18–21 167
Matthew 13 .... 18, 106, 114
Matthew 13:1–23 114
Matthew 13:14–15, 35 167
Matthew 13:24–43 116
Matthew 13:44–52 ...... 19, 118, 160
Matthew 13:47 52
Matthew 14:13 169
Matthew 14:13–21 .... 120, 176
Matthew 14:22 169
Matthew 14:22–33 122
Matthew 14:27 173
Matthew 15:21–28 ...... 19, 124, 174
Matthew 15:32–39 176
Matthew 16:13–20 128
Matthew 16:13–27 66
Matthew 16:21–27 130
Matthew 16:16 122
Matthew 16:22 122

Matthew 17:1–9 66
Matthew 17:7 173
Matthew 17:22–23 130
Matthew 18 136
Matthew 18:3–5 .... 112, 172
Matthew 18:6 172
Matthew 18:1–7 18
Matthew 18:15–20 136
Matthew 18:21–35 138
Matthew 19:13–15 .... 112, 172
Matthew 20:1–16 140
Matthew 20:17–19 130
Matthew 21:4–5 167
Matthew 21:15 .... 112, 172
Matthew 21:28–32 142
Matthew 21:33–43 144
Matthew 22:1–14 148
Matthew 22:15–21 150
Matthew 22:22 152
Matthew 22:33 152
Matthew 22:34–40 152
Matthew 22:37–38 158
Matthew 22:40 .... 58, 170
Matthew 22:46 152
Matthew 23:1–12 154
Matthew 24:19 176
Matthew 24:37–44 24
Matthew 24:40–41 175
Matthew 25 176
Matthew 25:1–13 158
Matthew 25:14–30 160
Matthew 25:31–46 162
Matthew 26:6–13 19

Matthew 26:14–27:66.................. 74
Matthew 26:26–29...................... 120
Matthew 26:69–75...................... 122
Matthew 27:9 167
Matthew 27:55–56....................... 19
Matthew 27:62–66; 167
Matthew 28:1–10...................... 78
Matthew 28:5 173
Matthew 28:9–20...................... 167
Matthew 28:10 173
Matthew 28:16–20...................... 92
Matthew 28:19.............................. 18

Luke 1:11–20.............................. 168
Luke 1:26–38............................... 28
Luke 1:39–56............................. 126
Luke 2:1–14............................35, 36
Luke 2:15–20..........................35, 38
Luke 24:13–35 84

John 1:3, 10...................................... 96
John 1:1–18 .... 35, 42, 88
John 1:29–34............................... 50
John 3:1–21 171
John 3:16–18............................... 96
John 4:5–42 .... 68, 170

John 6:51–58................................... 98
John 9:1–41 70
John 10:1–10............................72, 86
John 10:10 72
John 11:1–45 72
John 14:1–12............................... 88
John 14:15–21............................. 90
John 14–17................................... 90
John 14:16................................... 171
John 14:26........................... 94, 171
John 15:26.................................. 171
John 16:7 171
John 16:13 94
John 20:1–9................................. 80
John 20:19–31.............................. 82
John 20:19–23.............................. 94
Acts 8:30–31...................................8
Romans 1:19–20.......................... 174
Romans 13:14.................... 134, 175
1 Corinthians 3:16 152
1 Corinthians 12 136
Galatians 3:27–28....................... 175
Colossians 3:12, 14...................... 149
Hebrews 4:12................................. 13
1 John 2:1 171

Endnotes

1   *Gaudium et Spes*, 'Pastoral Constitution on the Church in the Modern World', Vatican II, 1965, 4.

2   Dietrich Bonhoeffer, quoted in Berry and Mobsby, *A New Monastic Handbook, From Vision to Practice*, London: Canterbury Press, 2014, p. 1.

3   Pope Francis (@Pontifex), 'The words of Sacred Scripture ... ', Twitter, 28 January 2021, https://twitter.com/Pontifex/status/1354768690949009410, accessed on 6 February 2021.

4   Thomas Keating, *Intimacy with God*, New York: Crossroad 1994, p. 164.

5   Matthew's Gospel depends heavily on Mark's Gospel for material. Almost ninety per cent of Mark's Gospel is in Matthew, therefore scholars state that Matthew cannot be dated earlier than AD 80; considering that Mark was written in Rome around AD 70, one must allow 'for a certain dissemination of Mark away from its place of origin'. Brendan Byrne SJ, in *The Paulist Biblical Commentary, Matthew*, New York: Paulist Press, 2018, p. 900.

6   Scholars offer several reasons for this assessment. Firstly, an eyewitness would not rely so heavily on another source (Mark) and would more than likely mention they are an eyewitness to these events. Secondly, this Gospel is written in Greek style and does not appear to be a translation from Aramaic or Hebrew. Finally, the dating of the Gospel to the final quarter of the first century means that Matthew the apostle would most likely have died by then. Ibid, pp. 900–901; Daniel J. Harrington, *The Gospel of Matthew*, Collegeville, Minnesota, 1991, pp. 8–9; Donald Senior, *Matthew*, Abingdon New Testament Commentaries, Nashville, TN: Abingdon Press, 1998, p. 22.

7   Anna Case-Winters notes that the evidence for the place of writing points to a prosperous, Greek-speaking urban area with a large Jewish population. Antioch would fit this description. Also the Bishop of Antioch, Ignatius, uses Matthew's Gospel as early as AD 107 which would suggest that it was well known in that region by then. Anna Case-Winters, *Matthew: A Theological Commentary on the Bible*, Louisville, KY: Westminster John Knox Press, 2015, pp. 20–21.

8   The Jewish historian Josephus recounts this landmark event in his work *The Jewish War* and a fascinating summary is given in Harrington's commentary, *The Gospel of Matthew*, p. 10 ff.

9   Harrington, *Gospel of Matthew*, p. 12.

10   Texts that are unique to Matthew's Gospel include the infancy narratives (chapters 1–2) and the events following the discovery of the empty tomb (27:62–66, 28:9–20).

11   These include 1:22, 2:15, 23; 4:14–16; 8:17; 12:18–21; 13:14–15, 35; 21:4–5; 27:9

12   Senior, *Matthew*, p. 22.

13   Case-Winters, *Matthew*, p. 21.

14   A note on language may be useful here. The word 'kingdom' will be problematic for us today because it conjures up notions of empire and patriarchy. Language will always carry cultural baggage, especially when we are trying to describe something that is more a way of being than a physical reality. We use the phrase 'kingdom of heaven' in this book to stay faithful to the Scripture text, while also acknowledging the linguistic baggage.

15   Elaine M. Wainwright, 'Tradition Makers/Tradition Shapers: Women of the Matthean Tradition', *Word & World*, Volume XVIII, Number 4, Fall 1998. p. 383.

16   Richard Rohr, 'Advent Love Coming to Fullness', New Creation (online magazine), Centre for Christogenesis, 19 December 2016, https://christogenesis.org/love-coming-to-fulness/, accessed on 10 April 2022.

17   His dress is similar to that of Elijah, an Old Testament prophet (2 Kings 1:8) who was predicted to return to inaugurate the new age.

18   Ilia Delio, *Coming to Be Love*, Reflection for All Saints Day, 1 November 2017, for the Centre for Contemplation and Action, https://cac.org/coming-to-be-love-2017-11-01/, accessed on 21 February 2022.

19   Joan Chittister, *Woman Strength: Modern Church, Modern Women*, Kansas City: Sheed & Ward, 1990, p. 49.

20   According to a first-century Jewish historian called Josephus, it is likely that Herod had John killed because of his growing popularity and the threat of the political upheaval he posed. Case-Winters, *Matthew,* p. 70.

21   Austen Ivereigh and Pope Francis (co-authored), *Let Us Dream*, New York: Simon and Schuster 2020, p. 113.

22   Matthew's is the only Gospel to offer an explanation for the name Jesus: the name comes from the Greek form of the Hebrew name Joshua, which is derived from *yasha,* meaning 'he saves' or 'YHWH saves'.

23   Frederick William Robertson in Kerr Boyce Tupper (ed.), *Robertson's Living Thoughts*, Chicago: S.C Griggs and Company, 1881, p. 188.

24   Some examples in the Hebrew Scriptures include Abraham (Gen 15:12–21), Jacob (Gen 28:10–22), Joseph (Gen 37 and 40–41) and Samuel (1 Sam 3:3–14); and in the Gospels Zechariah (Lk 1:11–20), Joseph (Mt 1:20–21 and 2:13–22) and the wise men (Mt 2:12).

25   L. R. Knost, quoted in Mary Bea Sullivan, *Living the Way of Love: A 40-Day Devotional*, New York: Church Publishing, 2019, 90.

26   Taylor Caldwell, 'My Christmas Miracle' in Joe Wheeler (ed.), *Christmas in My Heart*, New York: Guideposts, 1996, p. 214. The story first appeared in *Family Circle* magazine, 14 December 1961.

27   Ishmael Beah, *A Long Way Gone: Memoirs of a Boy Soldier*, Sarah Crichton Books, 2008.

28   Pope Francis, *Fratelli Tutti: On Fraternity and Social Friendship*, Vatican: Holy See, 2020, www.vatican.va/content/francesco/en/encyclicals/documents/papa-francesco_20201003_enciclica-fratelli-tutti.html#_ftn109.

29 For a wonderful reflection on the story of our universe, we would highly recommend Brian Swimme & Mary Evelyn-Tucker, *Journey of the Universe*, New Haven, CT: Yale University Press, 2011, which weaves the findings of modern science with various wisdom traditions and is an accessible, wonder-filled read.

30 Sally McFague, *Blessed are the Consumers: Climate Change and the Practice of Restraint*, Minneapolis, MN: Fortress Press, 2013.

31 Bill Wylie-Kellerman, *Seasons of Faith and Conscience: Explorations in Liturgical Direct Action*, Eugene, OR: Wipf and Stock, 2008.

32 Joanna Macy and Chris Johnson, *Active Hope - How to Face the Mess We're in Without Going Crazy'*, California: New World Library, 2012.

33 Macy and Johnson, *Active Hope*, p. 32.

34 Pope Francis' audience with participants in the 20th World Congress of the International Association of Penal Law, 15.11.2019, https://press.vatican.va/content /salastampa/en/bollettino/pubblico/2019/11/15/191115j.html, accessed on 11/4/2022.

35 From Kabir Helminski (ed.), *The Rumi Collection: An Anthology of Translations of Mevlana Jalaluddin* Rumi, Boulder, CO: Shambhala Publications, 1999.

36 There are several instances of Jesus 'withdrawing' in Matthew's Gospel in response to threat or loss. For example, Jesus wishes to withdraw by himself after hearing of John's death (Mt 14:13). This attempt is thwarted by the crowds, but he later withdraws to the mountain 'by himself to pray' (Mt 14:22).

37 Matthew is quoting Isaiah 9:1–2 which refers to 'Galilee of the nations', a province which had been devastated by the Assyrian conquest of 721 BC when many Jews were taken into exile. Among its new residents were Phoenicians and Greeks, and immediately to the south was Samaria. At the time of Jesus' ministry it was a religiously and ethnically mixed province, and its mention here introduces Matthew's focus on Jesus' message being meant for both Jews and Gentiles.

38 Anne Frank, *The Diary of a Young Girl*, New York: Knopf Doubleday Publishing, 2010.

39 Deepak Chopra, *The Third Jesus: How to Find Truth and Love in Today's World*, London: Ebury, 2009.

40 A recording of Fannie Lou Hamer singing 'This Little Light of Mine' can be heard on her album *Songs My Mother Taught Me*. Her version of the song is also available on YouTube, https://www.youtube.com/watch?v=xhiV6DB_h_8, accessed on 6 May 2022.

41 Fannie Lou Hamer, quoted in *God's Long Summer: Stories of Civil Rights*, Princeton University Press, 2008.

42 Anna Case-Winters argues that Jesus fulfilling the law and the prophets can have several dimensions of meaning: '1. That Jesus brings into being what the law and prophets promised. Reference to the fulfilling of the law is often made just before Matthew quotes something from the Hebrew Bible. 2. That Jesus himself does what

the law and prophets in fact require of us. His life is moulded by the law, and it defines his vocation and the conduct of his life. 3. That Jesus teaches and lives the deeper meaning of the law, which is best understood in terms of the love command on which 'hang all the law and the prophets' (22:40). All the laws concerning tithing, ritual purity, and Sabbath observance remain in place, but they are subordinate to the love command. Love exceeds these. It requires more and not less than the law.' Case-Winters, *Matthew*, p. 84.

43   Brian Grogan SJ, *Where to From Here?: The Christian Vision of Life After Death*, Dublin: Veritas, pp. 66–67.

44   Elie Wiesel, 'The perils of indifference', Seventh White House Millennium, Washington, 12 April 1999, reproduced in Simon Sebag Montefiore, *Speeches that Changed the World*, London: Quercus 2005, pp. 216–217.

45   Montefiore, *Speeches*, p. 217.

46   The term was coined by the French spiritual writer Fr Pierre de Caussade SJ (1675–1751). His book *The Sacrament of the Present Moment* is a classic of spiritual teaching, encouraging abandonment to God and an awareness that we encounter God in everyday life.

47   Ron Rolheiser, *Daybreaks: Daily Reflections for Advent and Christmas*, Liguori, MS: Ligouri Publications, 2019.

48   Anne Thurston, *Because of her Testimony: The Word in Female Experience*, Dublin: Gill & Macmillan, 1995, p. 123.

49   The man's growth in faith is very similar to the progression/journey made by the Woman at the Well on the previous Sunday (Jn 4:5–42) who also grows in understanding of who Jesus is.

50   Akṣapāda, *The Analects of Rumi*, 2019, p. 87.

51   In John's Gospel 'the Jews' is used frequently to refer to Jesus' opponents. To today's reader this may seem anti-Jewish. That is not the case. It's important to remember that Jesus himself was Jewish, as were the disciples. What we have here is a disagreement within Judaism with regard to who Jesus really is. Some religious leaders accepted Jesus as Messiah, others did not. John is writing 70 years after the Jesus event, so 'The Jews' is not necessarily referring to Jesus' contemporaries but to the leaders who are opposed to the new Christian movement at the end of the first century and also to those who opposed Jesus during his earthly life.

52   John Dear, *Lazarus, Come Forth!: How Jesus Confronts the Culture of Death and Invites Us into the New Life of Peace*, New York: Orbis Books, 2011, p. 5.

53   Quoted in Daniel S. Brown Jnr (ed.), *A Communication Perspective on Interfaith Dialogue: Living with the Abrahamic Traditions*, Plymouth: Lexington Books, 2013, p. 17.

54   Alan E. Lewis, *Between Cross & Resurrection: A Theology of Holy Saturday*, Grand Rapids, MI: Wm. B. Eerdmans Publishing Co., 2001, p. 3.

55 Fra Giovanni Giocondo, in a letter to his friend Countess Allagia Aldobrandeschi on Christmas Eve, 1513.

56 Jeremiah Wright, 'Wright's "Audacity to Hope" Sermon', *The New York Times*, 30 April 2008, https://www.nytimes.com/2008/04/30/us/politics/30text-wright.html, accessed on 9 May 2022.

57 Daneen Akers, 'What if Jesus came to live, not to die?', www.holytroublemakers.com /blog/nonviolenteasterbooks, accessed on 18 July 2022.

58 Shane Claiborne, *The Irresistible Revolution: Living as an Ordinary Radical*, Grand Rapids, MI: Zondervan, 2006, p. 150.

59 Joan Chittister, *Vision & Viewpoint*, Easter 2022, https://mailchi.mp/benetvision/do -no-harm-to-the-earth-749757?e=a677af4d17, accessed on 18 April 2022.

60 Pope Francis, 'Homily of Pope Francis', Saint Peter's Basilica Homily, Holy Thursday, 28 March 2013, www.vatican.va/content/francesco/en/homilies/2013/documents /papa-francesco_20130328_messa-crismale.html.

61 Jim Deeds (@gymforthesoul), Twitter, 31 March 2022, accessed on 1 April 2022.

62 Richard Rohr, *Dying into Life*, Homily for Tuesday 5 July 2016, available from https://cac.org/dying-into-life-2016-07-05/, accessed on 29 March 2022.

63 Παράκλητος/*paraklētos* – Advocate is found only in John 14:16; 14:26; 15:26; 16:7; 1 John 2:1.

64 Joseph Whelan SJ, *Finding God in All Things: A Marquette Prayer Book*, Milwaukee, WI: Marquette University, 2009. This reflection is often attributed to Pedro Arrupe SJ.

65 William Loader, *The Gospel of Matthew: An Introduction for Preachers*, revised edition 2004, Bill Loader's Home Page (website), https://billloader.com/matt.html, accessed on 27 April 2022.

66 Pope Francis, 'General Audience', St Peter's Square, 17 April 2013, www.vatican.va /content/francesco/en/audiences/2013/documents/papa-francesco_20130417 _udienza-generale.html, accessed on 28 March 2022.

67 See Genesis 2:7, 'Then the Lord God formed man from the dust of the ground, and breathed into his nostrils the breath of life; and the man became a living being'; and Ezekiel 37:5, 'Thus says the Lord God to these bones: I will cause breath to enter you, and you shall live.'

68 Mark Patrick Hederman, *Underground Cathedrals*, Dublin: Columba 2010, p. 11.

69 Hederman, *Underground Cathedrals*, p.10.

70 While this exchange (Jn 3:1–21) takes place between Nicodemus and Jesus, Nicodemus may represent a group of people: Nicodemus introduces his first question with 'we know' (3:2) and Jesus addresses him with the plural Greek word for 'you' (3:7, 11, 12).

71 Richard Rohr, 'Jesus in the Trinity', adapted from Richard Rohr, *Immortal Diamond: The Search for Our True Self*, San Francisco: Jossey-Bass, 2013, pp. 98, 119–120, https://cac.org/jesus-in-the-trinity-2022-01-10, accessed on 18 April 2022.

72   Daniel J. O'Leary, *Travelling Light: Your Journey into Wholeness*, Dublin: Columba, 2001, p. 99.

73   O'Leary, *Travelling Light*, pp. 98–99.

74   Vincent Havner, *Hearts Afire*, CreateSpace Independent Publishing Platform, 2014, p. 56.

75   Corrie Ten Boom, *Clippings from my Notebook,* Nashville, TN: Thomas Nelson Inc, 1982, p. 33.

76   Verna J. Dozier, *The Dream of God: A Call to Return*, New York: Church Publishing, 2006, p. 109.

77   Joan Chittister, *God's Tender Mercy: Reflections on Forgiveness,* New London, CT: Twenty-Third Publications, 2010, p. 10.

78   In 2021 Pope Francis told cardinals that it was time to 'discard the trappings of our roles, our social recognition and the glitter of this world' and to adopt humility, *National Catholic Reporter*, www.ncronline.org/news/vatican/pope-francis-pleads -humility-pre-christmas-speech-vatican-officials.

79   Pope Francis listed 15 spiritual diseases that he felt had become endemic in the Vatican, hampering their work, amongst them 'spiritual Alzeihmers' and accused his hearers of living in 'parallel worlds', *National Catholic Reporter*, https://www.ncronline .org/news/vatican/pope-issues-scathing-critique-vatican-bureaucracy-pre-christmas -meeting.

80   Ivereigh and Pope Francis, *Let Us Dream*, p. 57.

81   Mick Heaney, 'My father's famous last words', *The Irish Times*, 12 September 2015, https://www.irishtimes.com/life-and-style/people/mick-heaney-my-father-s-famous -last-words-1.2348525, accessed on 7 March 2022.

82   Joyce Rupp, *Out of the Ordinary, Prayers, Poems and Reflections for Every Season,* Notre Dame, IN: Ave Maria Press, 2000, p. 211.

83   See Matthew 18:6 where the expression 'little ones' is also used: 'If any of you put a stumbling block before one of these little ones who believe in me...'

84   Pope Francis, *Laudato Si',* 230.

85   Pope Francis, *Laudato Si',* 231.

86   Later in the Gospel when Jesus is asked who is the greatest in God's kingdom, Jesus puts forward a child (18:3–5; 19:13–15). As Jesus enters Jerusalem it is the children who cry out in the Temple, '*Hosanna to the Son of David*' (21:15).

87   Hollis Miller, '15 Nuggets of Wisdom from Kids that Prove they are Wise Beyond their Years', Huffpost (website), 2 November 2015, https://www.huffpost.com/entry/wisest -things-your-kids-said_n_55e6f471e4b0c818f619c787, accessed on 17 March 2022.

88   *The Message* is a modern translation of the Bible by Eugene Paterson who wanted to translate the Bible from its original Greek and Hebrew into contemporary English in a manner that would convey the passion and excitement of the text for his students. Considered unconventional by some, it is a translation that uses American slang and is

an interesting approach. This quote is *The Message* translation of Matthew 11:28–30. You can read more about this translation here: https://www.biblegateway.com/versions/Message-MSG-Bible/.

89 'At its simplest the parable is a metaphor or simile drawn from nature or common life, arresting the bearer by its vividness or strangeness, and leaving the mind in sufficient doubt about its precise application to tease it into active thought' C.H. Dodd, *The Parables of the Kingdom* quoted in Senior, *Matthew*, p. 146.

90 We have here the parable which Jesus told of the Sower and then the explanations of the parable. Biblical scholars assign the origin of these explanations to the early Christian communities, therefore it is thought that these explanations were added to the text of Matthew's Gospel by the early Church.

91 Wendell Berry, *The Unsettling of America: Culture and Agriculture*, Berkeley, CA: Counterpoint Press, 2015 edition.

92 Jose A. Pagola, *The Way Opened Up by Jesus: A Commentary on the Gospel of Matthew*, Miami, FL: Convivium Press 2012, p. 132, quoted in Case-Winters, *Belief: A Theological Commentary on the Bible: Matthew*, Louisville, KY: Westminster John Knox Press 2015, p. 455.

93 Stanley Hauerwas, *Matthew: The Brazos Theological Commentary on the Bible*, Grand Rapids, MI: Brazos Press, 2006, p. 133.

94 Case-Winters, *Matthew*, p. 445.

95 Daniel Berrigan SJ, 'Bread', Value of Sparrows (website), https://thevalueofsparrows.wordpress.com/2014/11/21/mysticism-bread-by-daniel-berrigan/.

96 Variations of the words 'Do not be afraid' are repeated often in Matthew's Gospel: Mt 1:20, 8:26, 10:31, 14:27, 17:7, 28:5, 28:10.

97 Case-Winters, *Matthew*, p. 264.

98 Elaine M. Wainwright, 'Tradition Makers/Tradition, Shapers: Women of the Matthean Tradition', *Word & World*, Volume XVIII, Number 4, Fall 1998, p. 384. Wainwright undertakes here a creative imagining of this text, an ongoing story telling of an ancient story, in this instance she writes in the voice of the Canaanite Woman.

99 Catholic Women Preach brings the voices of diverse Catholic women to the proclamation of the Gospel through web-based resources. Following the liturgical year, Catholic women reflect on how the texts relate to all Catholics today with a special emphasis on the lives of women, their apostolic call, and their roles in the Church and the world. www.catholicwomenpreach.org.

100 Anne Thurston, *Because of Her Testimony*, p. 101.

101 Joan Chittister, *Woman Strength*, p. 23.

102 Caryll Houselander, *This War Is the Passion*, New York: Sheed & Ward, 1941, p. 32.

103 Bearing in mind that these texts were written decades after the crucifixion, the Gospel writers are trying to make sense of the scandal of a crucified Messiah.

104   Richard Rohr, *The Universal Christ, How a Forgotten Reality Can Change Everything We See, Hope for and Believe*, London: Society for Promoting Christian Knowledge, 2019, p. 148.

105   The term *Sensio Divina* has occurred in recent years as a way to describe *Lectio Divina with Nature*. There are many versions online, mostly adapted from this version written by Bruce Stanley of the Forest Church movement: http://www.mysticchrist.co.uk/blog/post/sensio_divina. We have decided to use *Lectio Divina with Nature* to describe this spiritual practice. We are very grateful to Fr. Séamus O'Connell for his insightful comments as we drafted this section on *Lectio Divina with Nature*.

106   'For what can be known about God is plain to them, because God has shown it to them. Ever since the creation of the world his eternal power and divine nature, invisible though they are, have been understood and seen through the things he has made' (Rom 1:19–20).

107   The process Jesus outlines has its roots in Jewish law, specifically Leviticus 19:17.

108   See also our reflection for the Second Sunday in Ordinary Time on page 50.

109   Dermot Farrell, *The Cry of the Earth, The Cry of the Poor – The Climate Catastrophe – Creation's Urgent Call For Change, A Pastoral Letter for the Season of Creation 2021*, Dublin: Veritas, 2021, p. 27.

110   The Ignatian Ecological Examen can be found here: http://www.ecologicalexamen.org/ and is a wonderful online resource to help people explore their relationship with God's creation. They have great resources for parishes too which could be incorporated into a group session or used as part of a penitential rite or service. http://www.ecologicalexamen.org/eco-examen-resources/.

111   *Laudato Si'*, 158. The first use of the phrase 'preferential option for the poor' can be traced to Fr Pedro Arrupe, superior general of the Jesuits, in a 1968 letter. It was later used widely by the bishops of Latin America and became central to the liberation theology movement.

112   *Laudato Si'*, 208.

113   To find out more about the palm oil industry and about more sustainable options, see https://www.fairtrade.org.uk/media-centre/blog/avoid-at-all-costs-why-sustainable-palm-oil-from-ghana-and-ecuador-is-the-future/ accessed on 9 May 2022

114   Those considered to be on the fringes of society are the ones who respond to Jesus' message, for example the wise men (2:1–12); the centurion (8:5–13); the Canaanite woman (15:21–28); and the many people in need of healing who approach Jesus.

115   Fiona Harvey, 'Major climate changes inevitable and irreversible – IPCC's starkest warning yet', *The Guardian*, 9 August 2021, www.theguardian.com/science/2021/aug/09/humans-have-caused-unprecedented-and-irreversible-change-to-climate-scientists-warn.

116   At an Interfaith gathering held in Glasgow in 2021, on the periphery of COP26 (the UN Climate Conference) Dr Rajwant Singh gave a presentation about his organisation Eco-Sikh www.ecosikh.org. This brilliant quote from Dr Singh became the

mantra of the week for hundreds of faith-based activists who were present in Glasgow.

117 Greta Thunberg, speaking at a climate strike in Berlin on 24 September 2021, in advance of COP 26 climate summit. Reported in https://www.theguardian.com /environment/2021/sep/28/blah-greta-thunberg-leaders-climate-crisis-co2-emissions, accessed on 27 April 2022.

118 The Laudato Si' Action Platform is a collaboration between the Vatican, an international coalition of Catholic organisations, and 'all men and women of goodwill' (*Laudato Si'*, 3) to bring healing to our common home. For more information on the Laudato Si' goals visit www.laudatosiactionplatform.org.

119 Sean McDonagh, *To Care for the Earth: A Call to a New Theology*, London: Geoffrey Chapman, 1986, p. 131.

120 St Francis, 'The Canticle of the Sun', https://catholicclimatemovement.global/wp -content/uploads/2015/08/CanticleOfCreatures.pdf, accessed on 20 April 2022.

121 Pope Francis, *Laudato Si'*, 11.

122 Also: Romans 13:14; Galatians 3:27–28.

123 Roger Harrabin, 'Pope warns oil bosses of climate threat', BBC News (website), www .bbc.com/news/science-environment-48641799.

124 Pope Francis, 'Address of his Holiness Pope Francis to Participants at the Meeting for Executives of the Main Companies in the Oil and Natural Gas Sectors, and other Energy Related Businesses', Vatican: The Holy See, Saturday 9 June 2018, www.vatican .va/content/francesco/en/speeches/2018/june/documents/papa-francesco _20180609_imprenditori-energia.html.

125 Pope Francis, 'Address of His Holiness Pope Francis to Participants at the Meeting for Executives of the Main Companies in the Oil and Natural Gas Sectors', 160

126 Thomas Merton, *Healing Our Violence through the Journey of Centering Prayer*, disc 5, Franciscan Media: 2002, CD. He continues: 'Love is all; not [love as] sentimentality, but love that is self-forgetful and free of self-interest.'

127 Cynthia Bourgeault, *The Wisdom Jesus: Transforming Heart and Mind – a New Perspective on Christ and His Message,* Boulder, CO: Shambala Publications, 2008, p. 29.

128 Urban Dictionary (website), https://www.urbandictionary.com/define.php?term =Do+As+I+Say+Not+As+I+Do, accessed 23 March 2022.

129 Daniel O'Leary, *Already Within: Divining the Hidden Spring*, Dublin: Columba 2007, p. 51.

130 Shane Claiborne & Tony Compolo, *Red Letter Christianity, Living the Words of Jesus No Matter the Cost,* London: Hodder & Stoughton, 2012, pp. 46–47.

131 The parable shows once again the Gospels' concern for women because their responsibility to be prepared and to be ready is the same responsibility placed on men in the preceding text (Ch. 24).There is also gendered pairing in the parables preceding this one (24:40–41) which depicts divine saving action, relative to men and to women.

In 24:19 we also see concern for women who are pregnant and nursing. Anna Case-Winters (p. 356).

132 If we feel dismayed by the allegorical portrayal of God in the parables we read these Sundays, that's ok. Remember, these are stories Jesus told to make a point. The parable works its magic by shaking us out of complacency, leaving us with questions and working on us as our week unfolds. Each of the parables in Matthew 25 is concerned with a character (a master or a bridegroom) who is 'away' or 'delayed' and then who suddenly returns, in this case 'after a long time'.

133 Marianne Williamson, *A Return to Love: Reflections on the Principles of 'A Course in Miracles'*, New York: Harper Collins, 1992, p. 190.

134 Matthew 11:5; 14:13–21; 15:32–39.

135 Case-Winters, *Matthew*, p. 365.